PLAY THEATRE COMPANY

POCKET PLAYS

OBERON BOOKS
LONDON

WWW.OBERONBOOKS.COM

First published in 2017 by Oberon Books Ltd
521 Caledonian Road, London N7 9RH
Tel: +44 (0) 20 7607 3637 / Fax: +44 (0) 20 7607 3629
e-mail: info@oberonbooks.com
www.oberonbooks.com

A catalogue record for this book is available from the British
Library.

PB ISBN: 9781786822611
E ISBN: 9781786822628

Cover design by Alexander Sullivan

Printed and bound by 4edge Limited, UK.

Visit www.oberonbooks.com to read more about all our books
and to buy them. You will also find features, author interviews and
news of any author events, and you can sign up for e-newsletters
so that you're always first to hear about our new releases.

Huge thanks to Philip and Christine at The Carne Trust,
for their geneorosity and support.

Contents

INTRODUCTION

PLAY began when I was offered free reign of a large, rarely used community hall in Camberwell. I was an actor - frustratedly waiting for auditions, working multiple 'money jobs', eager to create something of my own - but with no experience of producing. The space would fit (ambitiously) 150 people, if we crammed everyone in, and so I began racking my brains. I'd been to scratch nights in London, I'd been to 24 hour plays and whilst they both had elements of what I was interested in, they weren't quite right. So, I assembled the first company of 4 writers, 4 directors and 10 actors and we set about making something a bit different. Something fresh and new, and collaboratively devised, but also something slick and formed, and exciting for our audiences.

Thus began the PLAY process. A bit like Anthony Neilson's 'extreme theatrical sport', the rehearsal period is fast-paced, energetic and largely fuelled by biscuits. Over the two weeks that followed the four companies (each with 1 writer, 1 director and 2/3 actors) improvised, devised, wrote, re-wrote, and improvised some more and at the end of it we had four brand-new plays plucked from the minds of our creative teams. The important bit - and the bit that's stuck with us through every PLAYtime - is that every person in the room brings something to the plays we make. We start with nothing and end with…well, you can read on for yourself.

On an unbearably hot evening in 2015 - when I was convinced the world would be in the park drinking beers - we packed an unexpectedly large audience into an old community hall. Since then we've taken this process and performed our PLAYs at Hackney Showroom, The Old Red Lion Theatre, VAULT Festival, Pleasance Theatre and Paines Plough's Roundabout at the Edinburgh Festival Fringe. We've worked with over 150 supremely talented creatives and produced 30 brand new PLAYs.

I'm absolutely thrilled to bring a little selection of them to you, so that you can have a PLAY around with them for yourself.

Rebecca Durbin, Artistic Director

PLAY 8

PLAY 8 was first performed at the Old Red Lion Theatre in September 2015. It was later commissioned to be developed into a full-length production, *Clay*, that was performed at the Pleasance Theatre in April 2016.

WRITER

Adam Foster

Fear & Loathing (Kevin Spacey Foundation Award Winner 2016), *The Daily Plays* (Pleasance Islington), *Molly* (Charlie Hartill Fund for Theatre winners 2015), *Long Story Short* (Pleasance Islington/Charing Cross Theatre), *Broken News* (New Wimbledon Studios), *Matador(a)* (with Susan Kempster, Camden People's Theatre/Pleasance Islington/ BAC), *To-Do List* (CentreStage/MacMillan Cancer), *Clay* (Pleasance Islington), *Food Porn* (NYT), *Snow or (How Not To Tell A Joke)* (with Susan Kempster, The Place/Union Theatre Liverpool), and *Lucy* (with Susan Kempster, Camden People's Theatre). Adam graduated from Royal Holloway's MA in Playwriting with Distinction. He is writer-in-residence for Squint.

DIRECTOR

Hannah Hauer-King

Fury (Soho Theatre), *Brute* (Soho Theatre), and *Dry Land* (Jermyn Street Theatre). Other work includes: *Clay* (Pleasance Theatre), *PLAY 25* (Vaults Festival), and *Pool (No Water)* (Nomadic Theatre, DC).

As associate director: *Romeo & Juliet* (Shakespeare's Globe), *Titus Andronicus* (Greenwich Theatre, Edinburgh Fringe).

Hannah was resident assistant director at Soho Theatre in 2014. She is Artistic Director and co-founder of all female theatre company Damsel Productions.

CAST

Katharine Drury

Katharine trained at the Guildhall School of Music & Drama.
Theatre includes: *Prometheus Bound* (Sound Theatre), *Still Life*
(Old Red Lion), *The Merry Wives of Windsor* (BOAT), *Clay*
(Pleasance Theatre), *A Midsummer Night's Dream* (UK Tour),
and *Generation Ellipsis* (PLAY Theatre Company). Katharine is
now the producer of PLAY Theatre Company.

Alex Hope

Alex trained at Royal Welsh College of Music and Drama.
Theatre includes: *Half A Sixpence* (Chichester Festival Theatre
& West End), *Clay* (Pleasance), *Rapunzel* (PARK Theatre), and
History Boys (UK Tour). Television includes: *Outlander* (STARZ)
and *August 1914* (BBC). Alex is an associate at Thrive Theatre.

AUTHOR'S NOTE

Lines proceeded by character names should be spoken
as direct address to the audience.

A dash (-) proceeding a line indicates dialogue.

A dash (-) at the end of a line indicates an interruption.
The subsequent line should be spoken immediately afterwards.

A dash (–) or an ellipses (…) during a line
indicates a break in thought.

An ellipses (…) on its own indicates
a character deliberately remaining silent.

A slash (/) marks the point of interruption
in overlapping dialogue.

Some sentences lack concluding punctuation
to indicate that the speaker does not finish the sentence,
voluntarily or involuntarily.

Italics mid-sentence denote emphasis.

JORDAN: I'm in a room. A grey walled room. I'm in a grey walled room on a hard backed chair with a man who knows my name but has neglected to tell me his. A policeman. He looks like a policeman. To be fair, he has already told me he is one but he *looks* like one as well. The way he holds himself. The way he –

– Jordan?

JORDAN: He wants me to tell him what I saw. He wants me to tell him, in detail, exactly what I saw.

– Don't worry about being too specific

JORDAN: He says.

– Don't worry about boring me. You won't bore me. You can't bore me. Nothing you can say will bore me in any way whatsoever. Just tell me. Just tell me exactly what happened.

JORDAN: I know this is difficult. He says, pushing for a response. I thought I'd responded already but clearly I hadn't.

– I know this must be extremely difficult for you –

JORDAN: He says

– but we do need you to tell us. We need you to tell us so we can find them. We need you to tell us, in detail, exactly what you saw so we can find the person, the people, who did this.

JORDAN: Medium height, I say, as if that information will be of any use whatsoever.

– Male?

JORDAN: Male, yes. Tall. Maybe…6'3"? Black hair. A beard. Not a beard so much as stubble. Off-white top. And dark trousers. That is the description I give. That is the description I give of the person who did this to her.

*

LINDSAY: I see him from across the room. He's talking to someone. A friend, it looks like. He's talking to a friend in a crowded room at a house party in Bromley when I see him look over at me.

JORDAN: She does this thing with her mouth. Not like that. When she's – I don't know – when she's somewhere she hasn't been before. Somewhere unfamiliar. Or if she's nervous or uncomfortable or in any way apprehensive. She puts her tongue on one of teeth. On her lateral incisor. This one. I looked it up. She puts her tongue on her lateral incisor and she feels the sharpness of it. I think. I think that's what she does. I obviously don't know for certain what she does because – well, because how could I? Really. But I'm guessing that's what she does. I'm guessing she feels how sharp it is. Or how smooth it is. Or how furry it is if she hasn't brushed her teeth in a while. She does this when she's nervous. When she's somewhere she hasn't been before. And she's doing it, now, in the lobby of –

LINDSAY: I remember his eyes. I remember looking in his eyes and for some reason having this sudden wave of – I don't know – something. And smiling. I must have smiled because now he's smiling back at me.

JORDAN: The hotel lobby is all wood and chrome and marble. A man – a boy really, no older than fourteen – takes our suitcase. I tell him not to worry. I tell him not worry but he insists. He won't take no for an answer.

LINDSAY: And then we're talking. We're talking and we're laughing. We're talking and we're laughing and we're doing that thing where we're trying to be the absolute very best version of ourselves. And it's working. From what I can tell, it's working.

JORDAN: The boy from the lobby drops our suitcase outside our room. And when I say drop I do mean drop. He literally drops it. On the floor. I say thank you very much and hand him ten dinar. About three pounds. And he cups my hand and looks at me with a look of such warmth and gratitude that you'd think I just gave him a blank cheque or the keys to a Bentley. I don't have a Bentley. I will never have a Bentley.

LINDSAY: He starts telling me about his work. And it's not just that it's boring. It *is* boring. But it's not just that. The thing is, I sort of thought these two versions of ourselves were better than that. Better than small talk. I didn't think after – what? – less than five minutes these two very absolute best versions of ourselves would have to resort to small talk as a means of making conversation. So I go to leave.

– Where are you going?

– Get a drink. *(Beat.)* Want one?

– What?

– A drink. *(No response.)* Do you want me to get you a drink?

– I'll come with you.

LINDSAY: And after that he knows. He knows never to try small talk again for the rest of the evening. Or again. Ever. And we go back to being the very absolute best versions of ourselves. We go back to being exemplary human beings.

'Crazy Stupid Love' by Cheryl Cole might play at this point. LINDSAY and JORDAN might remain completely still. Or they might mime the lyrics. Or they might do something else entirely. Or the song might not play at all.

*

JORDAN: We're in our room. It's nice. It's a nice room.

LINDSAY: The room is shit. It's got shit walls, shit carpet, shit pictures on the wall and a shit view of a carpark.

JORDAN: I've always liked staying in hotels. There's something about the… I don't know the anonymity I guess. And I know a lot of people don't like thinking about the number of people who might have stayed there before you but I really like thinking about that. Is that weird?

LINDSAY: There is a window seat. Why is there a window seat? Why would anyone want to sit on a window seat and look at a view of a fucking carpark?

JORDAN: I think maybe it's because I'm not old enough to have been worn down by staying in hotels for business trips and conferences.

LINDSAY: And conference facilities. Why would anyone hold a conference here?

JORDAN: I walk up behind her. I walk up behind her in the room in our hotel and I put my hands around her waist. I do this thing I know she likes where I run my finger across the top of the front of her jeans. She's sweating a bit.

LINDSAY: It's hot. It's too fucking hot. And he's doing that thing I *fucking hate* where he puts his hands down my jeans a bit because he thinks it teases me or something but actually he usually just ends up scratching me with one of his hangnails.

JORDAN: I put my hands on her hips and turn her round to face me.

LINDSAY: Then he tries to kiss me. He tries to kiss me on the mouth but he misjudges it and kisses me, instead, on my chin. But what's weird is that he doesn't try to kiss me again. Not straight away. He doesn't try to correct it. He doesn't actually acknowledge in any way whatsoever the fact that he has just kissed me on my chin. Maybe he meant to. Maybe he meant to kiss me on the chin. Maybe that's what he intended. Maybe he –

JORDAN: I kiss her again. I kiss her again and put my tongue just a little bit inside her mouth because I know she likes that too.

– I don't want to have sex.

– What?

– …

– I wasn't –

– Just don't okay because I really don't want to.

– Yeah that's fine as I say I / wasn't even

– I'm hot and I'm tired and I –

– It's fine.

Long pause.

– Shall we unpack?

– What?

– Do you want to unpack now or in the morning?

– No, yeah, leave it for now

– I can do it now if you want?

– It's fine.

– I don't mind

– It's fine. Leave it.

– Actually I will just get my shirt out

– Jordan.

– Wonder if there's an iron

– Stop.

– What?

– Just because I don't want to have sex with you doesn't mean you have to suddenly unpack.

JORDAN: We used to have sex a lot. Like a *lot*. Arguably too much.

LINDSAY: I would actually quite like sex.

JORDAN: And we still do. Don't get me wrong we do still have sex.

LINDSAY: I would really actually like some sex. Just not with him. I just really don't want to have sex with him.

– I was trying to be honest and open and like that just didn't – yeah

– Fine.

Long pause.

– Congratulations. Your boyfriend – like every other person's boyfriend – watches porn

– That's not true

– It is true!

– Tacky lesbian porn? I don't think everyone else's boyfriend watches that.

– There's actually nuances in lesbian / porn that

– Nuances?

– Yes. I've discussed this with you before – like when we first got together

– We have never discussed the 'nuances' of / lesbian porn

– Well I've discussed it with someone

– Wasn't me.

Pause.

– I'm not about the story –

– I don't want to know.

– It's all about whether there's –

– I don't want to know

– Whether there's two people that look into each other's eyes on that video and have a connection –

– Do you know what, that is gross.

Slight pause.

– Why is it gross?

– That is so much grosser / than just –

– I think it's true

– beating off to porn instead of analysing – you're a fucking wierdo, Jordan.

Slight pause.

– I think a lot of people share that – like – desire to actually have like…to see some sort of connection

Long pause.

– I dunno, might be weird. *(Beat.)* I really want some gnocchi.

– Go on then…

Pause.

You are not going to talk me into having dinner with you.

– Okay, don't have dinner with me but do you want anything from Sainsbury's?

– No.

– Okay.

Pause.

– I have never heard anyone talk about porn like that. It's really, really strange and I don't know why you shared / that with me.

– Yeah right okay so I know you don't want to discuss it but if you think about what you're actually looking at –

– I really don't want to talk about it.

– Fine. Okay.

Cheryl Cole's 'Call My Name' from her 2012 album 'A Million Lights' plays. It is a banger.

∗

JORDAN: He tells me I'm going into too much detail. The policeman. He says he knows he said that I should go into as much detail as possible. But this is too much. This isn't relevant. This is not a relevant detail. He tells me to talk about the beach.

– What happened on the beach?

JORDAN: He says

– Tell me what happened on the beach.

∗

JORDAN: We have come to the beach. It is the morning now. It is our first morning here and we have come to check out the beach.

LINDSAY: The resort is shit. Like, I was expecting it to be shit but it is *so* much shitter than I expected.

JORDAN: We're not wearing any shoes.

LINDSAY: The beach is full of people who I have no doubt whatsoever enjoy watching Britain's Got Talent on ITV. Followed by Britain's Got More Talent on ITV2. Followed by –

JORDAN: We find a good spot. We find a spot on the beach where there are three vacant sunbeds. She puts her stuff on one. Her book and her sun cream and her handbag. I go to put my towel on the one next to her.

    – Don't.

JORDAN: She says

    – What?

    – Don't. Just –

JORDAN: She tells me to move it. My towel. She tells me there's no need for me to be that close to her. Not when there's three

    – If there was two then fine but there's three so

JORDAN: I have to admit she's been a bit like this since we got here. I'm not entirely sure why. I'm really not at all sure why she's being like this. I think about asking her. I think about asking her why she's being like this. I think about what words I would use. What words I would use to make it sound like I hadn't thought at length about every single word I'd chosen to say to her. But I don't. Of course I don't. I just say

    – Nice beach isn't it?

JORDAN: And she gives me a look of such disdain that I really wish I hadn't.

– Yeah.

JORDAN: She says

– It's alright.

JORDAN: Then she stands up and goes to leave

– Where are you going?

JORDAN: I say

– Get a drink.

JORDAN: She says

– Want one?

JORDAN: I notice that she's taking her phone with her. Why is she taking her phone with her?

– What?

– A drink.

JORDAN: I don't like drinking before midday. Is it just me? Is it just me or does drinking before midday make you feel a little bit homeless?

– Do you want me to get you a drink?

JORDAN: She says again. I thought I'd replied but clearly I hadn't.

– Jordan?

– Where are you going?

– Get a drink. *(Beat.)* Want one?

– What?

– A drink. *(No response.)* Do you want me to get you a drink? *(Beat.)* Jordan?

– Where are you going?

– Get a drink. *(Beat.)* Want one?

– What?

– A drink. *(No response.)* Do you want me to get you a drink? *(Beat.)* Jordan?

– Where are you going?

– Get a drink. *(Beat.)* Want one?

– What?

– A drink. *(No response.)* Do you want me to get you a drink? *(Beat.)* Jordan?

JORDAN: I tell her I don't. I tell her not to worry. She says she isn't worried, she's just asking if I want a drink. She says she'll see me in a bit.

– I'll see you in a bit.

Long pause. Like too long. It's uncomfortable.

*

– Jordan?

– Why does she keep doing that?

– Doing what, Jordan?

– Why does she keep going away like that?

– Jordan, I need you to think.

– Okay.

– Carefully. I need you to think very carefully.

– Carefully, okay.

– Is there anyone with a reason not to like her?

– I don't think so.

– You don't think so or you know so?

– No. I know. Yeah.

– There's no one who might want to hurt her in some way?

– No.

– No one from her past who you think might –

– No. Not that I know of.

– Because I'm going to be honest we're struggling with motive here.

– Motive?

– We're struggling to see why someone would do this to her without having a motive for doing so. It doesn't make sense.

– No.

– Can you see why we might think that?

– No, yeah, I agree. It doesn't make any sense whatsoever.

*

LINDSAY: Later, I'm lying next to him. I'm lying next to him when he does that thing where your whole body jolts just before you go to sleep. Apparently it's an evolutionary thing. Apparently it's an ancient primate reflex that makes your whole body jolt to make sure you're not falling out of a tree. But he isn't. He isn't in a tree. I doubt he's *ever* been in a tree. He's in bed next to me.

JORDAN: She thinks I'm asleep.

LINDSAY: When I'm completely certain he's asleep I get out of bed as quietly as I possibly can. I put on a pair of jeans and a top and my sandals and I shut the door behind me. He's been texting me all day. The man from the hotel bar. He's been saying he wants to see me again. He's been asking me to come downstairs. So I'm going. I'm going to see him.

JORDAN: I hear her shut the door. She's trying to be quiet. Why is she trying to be quiet?

LINDSAY: As soon I shut the door I am hit by this sudden feeling of freedom. Being out of that room. That shit fucking window seat room.

JORDAN: I put on some clothes. I put on some clothes and I follow her. I follow her out of the room, down the corridor until it opens up into a sort of hallway. She's taking the lift. I see her taking the lift and I know I can't get in the lift with her – obviously I can't get in the lift with her – so I find the emergency stairway.

LINDSAY: I get out of the lift and a wave of cool air hits me in the face as I make my way through the lobby to the hotel bar.

JORDAN: I feel like a spy. Like an international man of mystery spy. I lean back against a wall and pretend I've got a gun. I don't have a gun. I obviously don't have a gun.

LINDSAY: I can't see him. I was expecting him to be here already. I was expecting to walk in and see him standing there but I can't see him anywhere so I walk over to the bar and I order a double whisky and I have no idea why.

JORDAN: I come out of the emergency stairway and go through to the lobby. I smile at the boy who carried our suitcases. He doesn't smile back. I think he hasn't seen me so I give him a quick wave to get his attention but then I realise that he had seen me and had just chosen not to smile so now it's slightly weird and uncomfortable but I'm okay with that so I keep walking. And that's when I see her. She's ordering a drink. A whisky. Why is she ordering a whisky?

LINDSAY: I take my whisky and I find a quiet table in the corner of the hotel bar. There's a menu on the table. I sit and I read the menu. They do scampi.

JORDAN: She's reading a magazine and I start to feel terrible. Why have I followed her? She's on her own. She's completely on her own. She couldn't sleep and she's just having a quiet drink on her own and I have blown this completely out of all proportion and I am going to leave now because I am weird. I am fucking weird. And I am going to leave when a guy walks over to her and touches her on the small of her back. I think that's a very intimate thing for a waiter to do but they are a bit pervy here so. But then they're laughing. They're talking and they're laughing and I think maybe he's a friend from home but that doesn't make any sense.

LINDSAY: He's gorgeous. He looks absolutely gorgeous. He looks absolutely gorgeous and confident and he doesn't say a word. He doesn't have to. He just holds out his hand and I can't not take it can I?

JORDAN: I see them walk out of the hotel bar, through a metal gate and down onto the beach. They are holding hands. Why are they holding hands?

LINDSAY: It's dark and there's no one around. The moon is out. A big fat brilliant moon that leads us down to the ocean.

JORDAN: I'm realise I'm not wearing any shoes.

LINDSAY: He's drunk. Super drunk.

JORDAN: He gives her a beer.

LINDSAY: He hands me one of those beers with tequila in it. I down it in one. I get bubbles up my nose.

JORDAN: I have never seen her do that. I have never ever seen her neck a bottle of beer like that.

LINDSAY: I wish I was more drunk.

JORDAN: It's cold. I suddenly feel really cold. I wish I'd brought a jacket with me.

LINDSAY: Suddenly he just leans in and kisses me and it's like the easiest thing ever. He's a good kisser. But he doesn't make a thing of it you know? He just kisses me. And I let him. I just let him kiss me.

JORDAN: He's kissing her.

LINDSAY: I'm really, really horny.

JORDAN: It's passionate. From what I can tell, it is a passionate kiss.

LINDSAY: He undoes my jeans quite roughly and I push him back onto the sunbed.

JORDAN: She's sucking his dick. With her mouth.

LINDSAY: I take my jeans off but I leave my pants on because I quite like that to be honest with you. I pull my pants to one side and lower myself onto him and we fuck and we fuck and it is completely fucking brilliant.

JORDAN: This isn't like on the internet. There is a connection. They have an extraordinary connection. It is fascinating to watch.

LINDSAY: I can taste the beer on his lips.

JORDAN: I get a bit of semi.

LINDSAY: And then he bends me over the sun lounger and fucks me from behind until he pulls his dick out and comes all over my back.

JORDAN: She's never let me do that.

LINDSAY: We both laugh a bit.

JORDAN: They're laughing.

LINDSAY: And I say hi, I'm Lindsay.

JORDAN: They're talking / and they're laughing.

LINDSAY: And he laughs and we just sit there in this completely comfortable happy silence under this big fat brilliant moon and it's kind of lovely actually.

JORDAN: I am smiling. Why am I smiling?

LINDSAY: He says he's going to go back inside now. He's meeting his friends. He asks me if I want to come with him but I tell him I don't. I tell him I'm going to stay here actually. / And then he goes.

JORDAN: He goes but she doesn't go with him. She just sits there. She just stays sitting there on the sunbed with cum all over her back looking out at the reflection of the moon on the ocean. And I think about the number of people who have sat on sunbeds with cum all over their backs. Probably quite a few. I'm thinking of this when a man walks out of the shadows. This man – a tall man – with black hair, a beard, not so much a beard as stubble really, an off-white top and dark trousers. He's not wearing any shoes. He walks over to her, this man, and she looks like she's just seen Princess Di. She looks surprised. She looks like she knows him. She looks at him like they've met before. I think maybe he's a friend from home but that doesn't make any sense.

– That doesn't make any sense whatsoever.

JORDAN: She's angry now. She looks angry. In fact I know she's angry because she's shouting at him. She's asking him why he followed her. She's calling him a

– fucking weirdo

JORDAN: And he remains – somehow – still. He remains – through all this – completely still. She starts to hit him on the chest and, still, nothing.

– You're a fucking weirdo, Jordan.

JORDAN: She's saying

– You're really really fucking strange and I really wish I never met you

JORDAN: And I think what are the chances? What are the chances of him – this man on the beach – having the same name as me? What an extraordinary coincidence. What a completely extraordinary coincidence. And as I'm thinking this she goes to leave. She's always going to leave. Why won't you stay still? Why won't you just stay fucking still? And then he's grabbing her. He's grabbing her and he's grabbing her and I've got my hands around her throat and I am heady. I am dizzy. Her face divides and multiplies and I've got a noise in my head that sounds like a washing machine on full spin. And there's noise and there's hands and there's noise and there's hands and there's noise and there's hands and there's noise and there's hands and then she is still. She is completely still.

*

– Thank you, Jordan.

– What?

– I think we've got everything we need.

– You – I… I don't understand.

– What don't you understand?

– Am I – ?

– …

– Like can I just –

– What?

– Go?

– No, Jordan.

– No?

– No, you need to stay here. We need you to stay right here.

PLAY 12

PLAY 12 – *Not That Kind of Guy* was first performed at VAULT Festival in January 2016. It was later revived at the Edinburgh Festival Fringe for PLAY Around, as part of Paines Plough's Roundabout Season, in August 2016.

WRITER

David Mumeni

David is a writer and an actor. Writing work includes: *Our Days of Rage* (co-written for the Old Vic Tunnels), *Early Doors* (co-written for Not Too Tame/UK Tour), *Not In Nottingham* (Royal Stratford East), and *Hollie* (NYT/UK Tour). Acting work includes: *Lela & Co.* (The Royal Court), *Pine* (Hampstead Theatre), *The Machine* (Donmar/Manchester International Festival/New York Amory), and *'Tis Pity She's a Whore* (Cheek by Jowl). TV credits include: *Fearless* (ITV), *Love Nina* (BBC), *Cuckoo* (BBC3), *The Windsors* (Ch4), *Fresh Meat* (Ch4), *Drifters* (E4), *Phoneshop* (E4). Film credits include: Woody Harrelson's *Lost In London, Noble, The Inbetweeners Movie,* and *The Huntsman: Winters War.*

DIRECTOR

Kirsty Patrick-Ward

Exactly Like You (Festival Spirit Award, The Vaults 2017/ Edinburgh Festival 2016), *Chef* (Soho Theatre 2015/Fringe First Winner, Edinburgh Festival 2014), *People Like Us* (Pleasance), *Snow White* (Old Vic/Educational Tour), *Chavs* (Lyric Hammersmith), *Brave New Worlds* (Soho Theatre), and *Life Support* (York Theatre Royal).

As associate director: *Present Laughter* (Bath Theatre Royal), *Brideshead Revisited* (ETT), and *Communicating Doors* (Menier Chocolate Factory).

As assistant director: *Arcadia* (ETT), *King Lear* (Shakespeare's Globe), and *Othello* (Shakespeare's Globe).

Kirsty is Artistic Director of Waifs + Strays theatre company and took part in the National Theatre Studio Director's course 2015. She is currently a director for National Theatre Connections and also took part in the Old Vic New Voices TS Eliot US/UK Exchange in 2011.

CAST

Lewis MacKinnon

Lewis trained at The Oxford School of Drama and with the National Youth Theatre. Theatre includes: *Three Sisters* (Belfast Lyric Theatre), *Your Last Breath* (Southwark Playhouse), *Black Sheep* (Soho Theatre), and *Live Lunch: Kid A Kidder* (Royal Court). Television includes: *Victoria* (ITV), and *Doctors* (BBC). Film includes: *Dragonheart:Dragonborn* (Universal), *The Wyrd* (Raging Quiet), and *Chosen* (Sterling Pictures).

Assad Zaman

Assad trained at Manchester School of Theatre. Theatre includes: *Coriolanus* (RSC), *Salome* (RSC), *Arms and the Man* (Watford Palace), *A Midsummer Night's Dream* (New Wolsey Theatre), *East is East* (Jamie Lloyd Productions/ATG), and *Behind The Beautiful Forevers* (National Theatre).

Television includes: *Apple Tree Yard* (Kudos for BBC1), and *Cucumber* (Red Productions for Channel 4).

CHARACTERS

LAWRENCE

*28, Scottish, middle-class, trendy dressing, maybe even
specs. Appears confident.*

MATI

*25, Geordie, working-class, thinks in quick thoughts.
Can appear unknowing and unsure.*

LAWRENCE: She's tall

MATI: Quite Petite

LAWRENCE: Brunette

MATI: Blonde

LAWRENCE: Striking looking.

MATI: She's got massive… *(Beat.)* eyes.

LAWRENCE: Kind of beautiful and Amazonian, in a way.

MATI: Eyes! I was always going to say eyes. Blue. The piercing kind.

LAWRENCE: But very thin.

MATI: Cheeks you wanna squeeze.

LAWRENCE: Collar bone showing. Not in an unhealthy way. In a normal natural way.

MATI: Not like how my Khala used to squeeze them. 'He's gonna be so handsome when he grows up. All the girls will come after him.'

LAWRENCE: Which isn't normally my type. Not that I have a particular type, but a women doesn't have to be stick figure thin for me to be attracted to her. I'm not that kind of guy.

MATI: Used to hurt like shit.

LAWRENCE: If anything, it's unattractive. The real catwalk models, they're unattractive. Too androgynous looking for me. Not a curve or an ounce of fat on them. It's absurd.

MATI: Fucking killed actually.

LAWRENCE: Theory is, gay men run the fashion industry and they put what they find attractive in their clothes. That's why we have these models looking like young men or boys. Much resembling ironing boards.

MATI: She's got this short hair, kind of pixie like. And big, full lips. The ones you want to kiss all the time. And may become useful for other things, later on, if you know what I mean?

LAWRENCE: And I just think it's bollocks, the pressures women are under to look a certain way. The constant objectifying they have to deal with on a daily basis, not just in the media /

MATI: Fuck! Is that sexist. Can I say that? No. It's not sexist. *(Beat.)* Is it?

I just mean. She's really fucking fit. I want her like. When I saw her I got that feeling you get when you just want to reach out and kiss them, and touch their waist and squeeze their ass.

LAWRENCE: Builders in the streets wolf whistling. 'Alright darling' or 'Look at the arse on that'.

MATI: I wouldn't. I wouldn't just like do that. I'm not that kind of guy. But that's what your working towards I guess. Aren't you? To be able to touch her. Not even sleep with her. Just touch, kiss, squeeze. That's the urge you get. As a man.

LAWRENCE: I once heard a group of young boys say, and I know she heard them too, 'She looks like she can take a dick'.

LAWRENCE: Fucking disgusting! It made me sick. No thought of how she might feel. As she was walking home, on her own.

MATI: And I can't help that. That urge. Can I? It's not my fault, it's the way we're wired right?

LAWRENCE: And men in white vans! I just think it must have worked once. That once, a man beeped his horn and shouted something to a women walking on her way to work, and she said to herself, 'Yes, I'll have me some of that' and she got in. And so now they all do it. Even to schoolgirls, in school uniforms, who have no idea why the men are beeping.

Beat.

MATI: Her name is Eve. Her family's Irish, I think.

LAWRENCE: I think the worst thing about it is that they don't see it. A lot of men, now, that as a society we all on the whole agree rape is bad, beating women is bad, that men can't just do, and get away with whatever they want anymore, believe that everything's alright now, what's all the fuss about?

MATI: I'm guessing she likes the Asian persuasion. I hope so. Don't know why, but... I've always had this thing in my head that – ahh – that sometimes if a white girl dates me – that she's just – trying it out. The Asian thing. And that actually she's always gonna want a white guy. In the end. So maybe without realising, I try to be less Asian 'coz... But I know that that is probably me though. Stupid really.

LAWRENCE: There's a theory about racism, can't remember where I read it now but it says that we, as a society, have been racist for so long, it's so ingrained in us, that we can't see racism anymore. That unless people are being put into chains, or being told to go home, or lynched in the street, racism doesn't really exist, anymore. I think it's like that.

MATI: There's a few things I worry about actually. I worry I'm too skinny. Like not...big enough. That I'm not... Channing Tatum enough, you know. And they all like Channing Tatum don't they? The thing is, I run. And exercise quite a bit. But well, I just can't get big...but I'm toned so...

Weird, because it wasn't a thing for men before. Body image or whatever. And although they don't always admit it... I know I've certainly heard women say it… *(Beat.)* 'I like a man, man', and what they mean is a big, strong man. And maybe it's bad to say because it's kind of opposite to the idea of feminism, in a way, but actually they still want a man to – aaah! – be able to protect them… There, I've said it.

LAWRENCE: Her name is Alicia. She works at the production company we're co-producing this new Jack Whitehall sitcom with. I know, another one. And, yeah, so I asked her if she wanted to go for some tapas. There's this new Lebanese place in Stokey, and they do a sort of Lebanese tapas and cocktails.

MATI: I'd just come out of the gym, and she works in this café that does posh salads. It's nine quid for a tiny plate, but I'm trying to get my five a day. So I go in there quite a lot and, the owner was like, 'Do you know any rich, handsome men that Eve could go out with, she needs a boyfriend.' She laughs and looks at me. And I make a joke like 'Ah that counts me out then. I'm just a barman.' And she said, 'Well just handsome will do, what you doing tonight?'

LAWRENCE: She made a joke about how she doesn't date children. I smiled at her and assured her I was no child. I just look young. I'm actually older than her. I'm 26. I just look young. And she says, 'Like a Scottish Owen Jones?'

MATI: I was taken a back a little to be honest. Like we're the ones always making the moves aren't we? Having to do the asking out? So at first it's a surprise, but I liked it. I mean I told my mate Dean I asked *her* out but /

LAWRENCE: I'm not the kilt wearing, Kaber tossing, brave heart Scot. I'm not that. This is what I look like.

MATI: It's seven o'clock. Got my new Farah shirt on and spray on my Dior Homme, Dad brought it back from the duty free. He usually brings back t-shirts with massive logos I can only wear for pyjamas, but he did well this time. Think its important to smell good. Lads don't really wear after shave but I always get compliments on it, how I smell nice. It's manly isn't it? Makes me feel...classic *man-ey*.

LAWRENCE: I WhatsApp'ed her the address and said I'd meet her there. Spray a bit of deodorant under my pits, brush my teeth in the toilets at work, and leave.

MATI: I'm about to leave but take the shirt off again and do a few more press ups before I go. I never forget what this guy said at school, to do as many press-ups as you possibly can, until you can't do anymore. It makes you look a bit buffer before you go out.

LAWRENCE: Get in an Uber.

MATI: Get on the tube.

LAWRENCE: Turn on my spotify. The drivers quite cold. I want to play a bit of Jack Garret but I have a sudden need to impress him. And that my choice in music somehow determines my masculinity. It annoys me that I care. A quick search and I put on 'Juicy' by Biggie Smalls. He turns it up, laughs, and asks, 'How do you know about this? I wasn't expecting you to play this, you know.' I have his 'man'-spect.

MATI: It's rush hour but still I manage to find a seat. I lift up the bottom of my shirt ends and lay them back on my thighs, not wanting the shirt to crease.

LAWRENCE: 'Super Nintendo, Sega Genesis. When I was dead broke man, I couldn't picture this.'

MATI: Two, quite tall blokes are smiling and laughing and looking over. I don't know if it's at me. Maybe I look too dressed up? Is it too tight? Do I look gay? Fitted shirt, do I look a bit gay? And there's nothing wrong with being gay. It's just I'm not and I'm trying to get this girl to fancy me. Maybe gays the wrong word, but it's the word people use, which is fucking bad of course, but maybe they mean, not man-like.

LAWRENCE: We've moved on to B2K now. Girlfriend – Pied Piper Remix, 'I need a girlfriend. I need a girlfriend.'

MATI: I'm two minutes late. You should never keep a girl waiting. Outside a station has got to be the worst place for a woman to stand I reckon. I get on the escalator not knowing whether to ride them or walk up and risk getting a bit sweaty. I'll ride them.

LAWRENCE: I say bye to the driver and walk into the bar. It's pretty busy for Tuesday.

MATI: I tap my oyster, take a quick look at myself making sure a strand of hair hasn't flopped down on to my face making be look like a back street boy. 'I *don't* want it that way'.

LAWRENCE: And there she is.

MATI: / Fucking hell /

LAWRENCE: /Fucking hell /

LAWRENCE: A class act, it must be said.

Beat.

MATI: Fucking hell.

LAWRENCE: She looks great. Same black chiffon top and black jeans she was wearing earlier today at work, but she's put a bit of mascara on and something on her lips. And she's let her hair down.

MATI: She looks so fit. Those urges to just…touch her again. But I can't look overwhelmed. I can't look nervous. You have to look cool, calm, strong, and confident because that's what women like.

LAWRENCE: I give her a kiss on the cheek and I sit down opposite her. We order and initially talk about work.

MATI: Don't' know if it's right but I open the door for her and we walk in.

LAWRENCE: Our cocktails arrive and the waitress gets them the wrong way round and gives mine to her. Because it has fruit in it and I guess she thinks it looks a bit girly.

Well, I like lychee and I like watermelon. It's tastes nice. When did fruit become just for women and homosexuals?

MATI: It's this tapas Lebanese, cocktail place. I didn't know they did cocktails in the Lebanon. I didn't know they did tapas in the Lebanon.

LAWRENCE: Plus I'm not gay, I've tried it. I *was* drunk but I wanted to. I kissed a guy in a club, even let him tug me off in the toilets. It was cool. But no I'm not gay, and I won't be put in a box so I won't say I'm not straight either.

MATI: The waiter comes over and puts down cocktail menus on the table and asks us how we are, but he's kind of only looking at her when he says it. And he's tall, and quite big and bearded and muscular. An Arab Channing Tatum looking mother fucker.

LAWRENCE: Alicia starts playing with the end of her hair a little and being very sarcastic. She's in to me. I make sure I'm sitting back and not leaning forward. Me leaning back means she'll have to lean into me. Looks like I'm not too keen and makes her work a bit harder.

MATI: I pretend not to notice it. Don't want to seem jealous, weak. Weak is not sexy, not manly. I scroll the menu and I sort of want this lychee and watermelon one but don't know what Eve or Abdul Tatum might think of me. That's not racist, he told us his name was Abdul.

LAWRENCE: I'm leading the conversation, I'm asking all the questions, I'm having to, in some way, control events.

MATI: You sort of have to. Lead. You can't let it die; it's like keeping the ball up.

LAWRENCE: But a silence does occur, a tiny one, one you were hoping for and she looks directly into my eyes and she says, 'Ok, so you're, smart, funny, doing well, got your own place, seem to know what you want out of life, why are you still single then?'

MATI: And we're getting on really well. And she tells me how she's about to start a job at a women's refuge charity, a place where women can go if they've suffered domestic violence. She talks a lot about the wasters she's dated. She talks about how even in the charity sector women aren't getting equal pay and I agree with her, that it's messed up. I tell her I don't think I'm feminist and she asks, 'Do you believe in equality?' And I say of course, and she says, 'Well then, you're a feminist.' So, I guess I am. I'm a feminist. So I'm careful about my words, careful not to man-terrupt. And I'm sensitive and caring but I still feel, in some way, I have to be strong. That I have to seem ambitious, with strong values and represent some form of stability. But I'm only twenty five, and I don't *really* know what I want yet and there's a bloody economic crisis so me and my income are anything but stable. Why can't I be just as worried and as unknowing as you?

LAWRENCE: Why am I still single? I'm single because I choose to be. Because I don't believe in, his or hers, the ownership of another individual. She's *my* girlfriend, he's *my* boyfriend. I will not objectify a women in that way. I tell her this, and she likes it, likes the idea. Says she's never thought of it that way.

MATI: The evening comes to an end and she nips to the toilet and I watch her as she walks off. So fit. / The bill comes /

LAWRENCE: / The bill comes / a petite blonde with pixie hair walks past, on her way to the toilet. She's gorgeous. I reach for my wallet and take out my card.

MATI: Right, how is this going to work? I mean I want to pay. Would feel pretty stingy if I didn't but would she get offended?

LAWRENCE: We'll split it. I don't want her feeling she owes me anything or that she's indebted to me in anyway. And why shouldn't we half it? She earns just as much as I do, actually, probably more, and in no way am I threatened by that.

MATI: She's back.

LAWRENCE: She clocks the bill.

MATI: Flicks those eyes to me, then back to the bill and says, / 'I'll get it.' /

LAWRENCE: / 'I'll get it.' /

MATI: The ethnic side of me kicks in and I get that feeling in my gut that something's wrong.

LAWRENCE: 'Are you sure?'

MATI: I think back to all those times when I was younger watching my Dad and Uncle shoving money into the servers hand as they fought over who would pay the bill. The most generous man was the biggest man. But / 'Erm. Sure.' /

LAWRENCE: / 'Erm. Sure.' /

MATI: Abdul Tatum comes over, picks up the card and hands it me.

LAWRENCE: 'No, it's hers, actually'.

MATI: 'Actually could you use this one?' and I take out my card from my wallet. Eve just smiles and looks down.

Beat.

LAWRENCE: / We leave /

MATI: / We leave / We're standing outside still talking, eyes flickering all over the place.

LAWRENCE: The possibility of a kiss.

MATI: The urge! I want to.

LAWRENCE: She wants to.

MATI: Whatever we talk about comes to a natural end.

LAWRENCE: Some laughter.

/ We kiss /

MATI: / We kiss. / Those lips.

LAWRENCE: We kiss for quite some time

MATI: I even do a bit of touching. Just her waist really. She is fit. I get a bit self conscious at first because there's another couple nearby but they're making out too so fuck it. But now / its home time /

LAWRENCE: / It's home time /

MATI: We're waiting for the Uber she's just ordered.

LAWRENCE: Hers or mine?

MATI: It arrives. She opens the door to get in, stops and then says 'Would you like to come to mine? Have another drink or whatever?'

MATI makes a face.

LAWRENCE: I guess we're going back to hers.

MATI: Back at hers. Quite a small flat. Two bedrooms. She lives with a mate from Uni, who's asleep.

LAWRENCE: She has a vinyl player of course. She puts on some Otis Redding.

MATI: She makes us tea.

LAWRENCE: She cracks open a bottle of wine.

MATI: She looks a little nervous, looking up, then back to the floor. Shit this might happen.

LAWRENCE: No pressure.

MATI: This is gonna happen. I need to get out of my head.

LAWRENCE: But it's hard.

MATI: How can you get out of your head when there's this pressure to perform?

LAWRENCE: You want to keep your eyes closed when you're kissing, but you check in, check she's enjoying it.

MATI: We move to the bedroom.

LAWRENCE: What if I come to quick?

MATI: What if I take too long to come and she gets bored?

LAWRENCE: What if she doesn't come?

MATI: What if she feels she has to fake it?

LAWRENCE: What if I'm not big enough for her?

MATI: And in that moment, when your having a bit a trouble… and your on your fourth condom of the sess(h), that's when, well, *I* certainly do…feel, emasculated.

And she asks, is it her? Is there something wrong with her? No. Because that's like, the one thing that is expected of us. To stay hard.

LAWRENCE: Because all men are the same, we all think with our dicks and we all just want to fuck anything that moves and the one thing we can always do is be hard on demand. And if we can't we're not men.

MATI: And that…I would say… I reckon that is the thing that…that like, our whole manhood is judged on. Our masculinity. Our penises and our ability to perform.

LAWRENCE: The one thing I will say ladies is the first few times you ever have sex with a man, he is not with you, he is in his head. Because one of the biggest things…

MATI: The biggest things…

LAWRENCE: One of biggest things coursing through a man's mind when he first has sex with you is… / Is she going to tell everyone that you were a bag of shite! /

MATI: / Is she going to tell everyone that you were a bag of shite! / I need to get out of my head!

Beat.

We're now laying on the bed.

LAWRENCE: And I know it's my job to take control, be dominant.

MATI: I try not to go too heavy. I've learnt the kind of woman she is through the work she does. She doesn't like that kind of man.

LAWRENCE: I lift her off the bed and kiss her up against the wall.

MATI: Our clothes are off

LAWRENCE: Our clothes are still on.

MATI: It's happening. We're having sex.

LAWRENCE: It's not happening. We are not having sex.

MATI: It's going well, I'm being gentle and considerate. A gentlemen.

LAWRENCE: Her eyebrows furrow and she asks, 'What is this?'

MATI: But then she says, 'You can do what you like to me.'

LAWRENCE: Not this. We barely know each other. Really?

MATI: Wow! A bit of dirty talk. 'Take charge' she says. That, I was not expecting. From her. But cool. I can do that. So I do. I won't bore you with the gory details you bunch of perverts but it's going alright, like.

LAWRENCE: I tell her that 'It's just…it is what it is.' And she says, 'I'm not that kind of girl.'

MATI: I'm now on top, trying my best to please her. Taking charge, like she asked. But then suddenly she grabs my arm and says 'Choke me.' *(Beat.)* 'What?'

LAWRENCE: What does she mean? What's that kind of girl? A slut? A slapper? A whore?

MATI: 'Choke me. Just a little' What? What the fuck? I stop and slowly clamber off. That's a bit… Isn't it? I didn't know she was *that* kind of girl.

LAWRENCE: 'You want to have sex with me, and I want to have sex with you. And if I want to sleep with you that's ok, but you wanting to sleep with me makes you a slag?' What a load of shite. I hate the phrase, 'I'm not that kind of girl?' I say this to her and she pauses.

MATI: She sits up and recoils back. 'I'm not a slag' she says. I tell her 'I know that'. And of course I do. When I said that kind of girl, I just meant…I didn't think she wanted me to be… *that* rough. Don't get me wrong. I don't mind it. *(Beat.)* But I worry. I ask her, 'You working at that place… did someone ever hit you?'

LAWRENCE: 'Why are you single?' I've told her this. I explain the ownership of being with someone again but this time she doesn't understand and just...laughs.

MATI: She says. 'No you idiot. You really think if that ever happened I'd ask you to do something like that?'

LAWRENCE: 'Your full of it' she says. And I don't, I honestly don't know what she means. 'How many women have you slept with?'

MATI: 'I know I don't know you very well, but I feel I do' she says. 'I just feel...comfortable, enough, with you. I dunno, I trust you enough to be able to...let you... ask you that.'

LAWRENCE: She can't ask that. Imagine if I asked the same thing. Plus, I can't remember. Quite a lot I guess, yes quite a lot. 'You act like you're a man of the world' she says, 'That you're enlightened, you're some sort of feminist...' Which I am! I fucking am. 'But that ownership stuff, it's just so you can sleep with as many women as you like. You actually don't know what you're talking about. Sounds like your spieling stuff off of some blog.' *(Beat.)* 'You can leave now. I'll see you bright and early.'

MATI: She says it doesn't matter and I should forget it. 'You can leave if you want?'

LAWRENCE: And I do leave

MATI: And I don't leave. I'm not leaving.

LAWRENCE: An Uber comes in no time and suddenly, surprisingly; I'm my way home. Alone.

MATI: I get in, and scoot back over to her. She looks at me, embarrassment in her eyes, and I say, 'I get it.' And I do. 'A gentlemen in the streets, a tiger in the sheets, right?' I heard it on TV once I think. She laughs.

LAWRENCE: Fuck. She's right. What am I doing? What the fuck have I been doing?

MATI: 'Wanna go again?' I ask. She dips her head under my arm and nestles it into my chest. 'Maybe in the morning.'

LAWRENCE: What have I been doing?

MATI: I kiss her head covered in her pixie hair and say, 'You don't have to worry about me, you know? / I'm not that kind of guy.' /

LAWRENCE: / I'm not that kind of guy. / Am I?

PLAY 17

PLAY 17 – *Waste Land* was first performed at Hackney Showroom in June 2016, as part of PLAY's *1st Birthday Edition.*

WRITER

Tristan Bernays

Tristan is a writer and performer from London. Writing work includes: *The Bread and the Beer* (Soho Theatre/UK Tour), *Teddy* (Best New Musical at the Off West End Awards 2016/ Southwark Playhouse), and *Frankenstein* (Wiltons Music Hall). Tristan's new play *Boudica* will be performed at The Globe in September 2017.

DIRECTOR

Oliver Dawe

Dead Sheep (UK Tour), *Perfidious Lion* (Underbelly), *Pufferfish* (Pleasance), *Frau Welt* (Hackney Showroom), *The Dog, the Night and the Knife* (Arcola), *We Really Should Do Something* (Bush), and *Little Baby Nothing, Rules* and *After the Ball* (Theatre503) Oliver trained as a director at Drama Centre London. He is the co-founder of RIVE Productions and an Associate Director of Etch Theatre company.

CAST

Aaron Gordon

Aaron trained with the National Youth Theatre Rep Company in 2013. Theatre includes: *Tory Boys* (Ambassador's Theatre). Television includes: *New Blood* (BBC), and *Fight Night* (Ontroerend Goed).

Rebecca Durbin

Rebecca trained at the Royal Welsh College of Music and Drama. Theatre includes: *TRACY* (Underbelly, Edinburgh/ Old Red Lion Theatre), *Santa Trap* (UK Tour), *Afterlife* (PLAY/ VAULT Festival), *We Are Nowhere And It's Now* (PLAY/Old Red Lion Theatre), *Blister* (RWCMD in association with Paines Plough), and *The Hired Man* (NYMT). Rebecca is the founder and Artistic Director of PLAY Theatre Company.

Rehanna Macdonald

Rehanna trained at the Royal Welsh College of Music and Drama. Theatre includes: *The Last Queen of Scotland* (Stellar Quines/National theatre of Scotland/Dundee Rep), *My Name Is* (Tamasha Theatre Company), *If I Had a Girl* (Citizens Theatre/ Amina), *Early Doors* (Not Too Tame Theatre Company), and *Child of the Divide* (Buchar Boulevard). Television includes: *Teacup Travels* (CBeebies/Plum Films). Radio includes: *Dr Who* (Big Finish Productions).

CHARACTERS

JASON

LAURA

AIOFE

TIME

Winter

PLACE

Outside Skaw, the northern-most point of Scotland.

April is the cruellest month.

T.S. Eliot

Winter.

Evening.

The living room of a cottage in Skaw.

LAURA is passed out on the sofa under a blanket.

JASON is sat next to her. There are two cups of tea and a glass of water.

LAURA wakes with a start.

LAURA: Ah!

JASON: Laura?

LAURA: Fuck fuck –

JASON: Laura –

LAURA: Jesus fuck –

JASON: Are you –

LAURA: Jesus, Jesus fuck my – Fuck – I –

   ...

   Jase?

JASON: Hi.

LAURA: What –

JASON: Are you alright?

LAURA: What are you –

She tries to sit up. Suddenly feels sick.

LAURA: Oh Jesus, oh –

JASON: Here.

He gives her water.

LAURA: No.

JASON: Just –

LAURA: I –

JASON: Come on. You'll feel better.

She relents. She drinks.

JASON: Better?

She nods.

JASON: How you feeling?

LAURA: My head feels like a cunt.

JASON: Right.

LAURA: Jesus.

What the fuck –

JASON: You're alright. You're okay.

LAURA: What –

JASON: You've been asleep.

LAURA: Yeah, yeah I kinda – kinda –

JASON: Twenty six hours.

LAURA: What?

JASON: I thought you were dead at one point.

LAURA: Jesus. Fuck. Fuck was I –

JASON: You looked dead when you turned up.

LAURA: What?

JASON: My doorstep. Four in the morning, you just – kept
ringing –

LAURA: Jesus.

JASON: Burbling and that –

LAURA: I – I don't –

JASON: Like you were –

LAURA: I don't even remember – doing that, I – like –

JASON: Well, you did.

LAURA: Right.

JASON: So.

LAURA: ...

> Yeah – Yeah, sorry, I – I didn't – I didn't mean –
>
> You got a – a – an aspirin or summat? Some paracetamol or –

JASON: Sorry.

LAURA: It's just my head, me head feels – Feels like there's a fucking – nail between my eyes you know? There, just – there, just fucking –

JASON: No. Sorry.

LAURA: You haven't got anything?

JASON: Have some more water.

LAURA: No, I –

JASON: You're dehydrated.

LAURA: I –

JASON: You need to drink.

LAURA: Jase –

JASON: You need to –

LAURA: Alright, alright! I'll fucking – Fucking – I'll fucking drink, I – Jesus.

She drinks.

LAURA: What time is it?

JASON: Nearly seven.

LAURA: Jesus. So fucking dark, innit? 'S like a fucking –

I hate January.

JASON: I know.

LAURA: I mean, I fucking hate –

JASON: You cold?

LAURA: No, no it's alright, I –

JASON: Here.

LAURA: No it's okay, I –

He holds out a pink hoodie.

Signals for her arms.

After a moment, she holds out her arms.

He dresses her in the hoodie.

She lets him.

He finishes and steps back.

She smiles at him.

LAURA: Thanks.

JASON: S'alright.

LAURA: You're looking good.

You look – good.

How are you?

JASON: I'm good.

LAURA: Good. Good. That's good.

He hands her a cup of tea. She drinks. He watches her drink it.

She smiles.

LAURA: Three sugars.

He smiles.

She looks at the hoodie properly.

LAURA: It's a bit –

...

JASON: What?

LAURA: Pink. For you.

JASON: No, no it's not mine, it's – er –

LAURA: Who's is it?

JASON: Aiofe's.

LAURA: Who?

JASON: My girlfriend.

LAURA: Girlfriend?

JASON: Fiancée, actually.

LAURA: Fiancée? Holy shit, Jesus, fuck, you fucking – Look at you! Look at you, you fucking – Mister Big Man now, eh? Aren't you? Fucking –

JASON: Yeah.

LAURA: Fucking hell, you getting married, that's – that's amazing, man that's – That's proper adult stuff there now, man, proper – That's amazing that, that's –

JASON: Yeah.

LAURA: What happened to Chrissie?

JASON: What?

LAURA: Black girl, tall. She was at Mike's wedding with you when – I liked her. She –

JASON: We broke up.

LAURA: What? When?

JASON: Year and a half ago.

LAURA: Fuck? What happened?

JASON: Didn't work out.

LAURA: Jesus. You never told me.

JASON: You never asked.

LAURA: No. No, but – Shit, no I – Shit, shit sorry, dude, that – That sucks, I – I didn't know.

JASON: No.

LAURA: Sorry.

JASON: S'alright.

LAURA: But you're with Eva now.

JASON: Aiofe.

LAURA: What?

JASON: Aiofe, not Eva.

LAURA: Eefar?

JASON: Aiofe.

LAURA: Aiofe? Like – Fifa?

JASON: Yeah.

LAURA: Right.

So you're with – her now?

JASON: Yeah.

LAURA: So that's good.

Is that good?

JASON: Yeah. Yeah, it's good.

LAURA: Good. Good. That's good.

You're looking good.

JASON: You said that already.

LAURA: Yeah, yeah well it – It's difficult to know what to say,
innit? Turn up on your doorstep like a fucking – gibbering
idiot and – Don't see you in a year and –

JASON: Six months.

LAURA: What?

JASON: Year and six –

LAURA: 'As it been that –

JASON: Yeah.

LAURA: Jesus.

You didn't have to take me in, you know.

JASON: What else was I gonna do?

Enter AIOFE.

AIOFE: Hey.

JASON: Hey.

AIOFE: Are you –

JASON: Law, this is Aiofe.

AIOFE: Hi.

JASON: Ee, this Laura.

LAURA: Y'alright.

AIOFE: It's great to meet you, Laura.

LAURA: Yeah, yeah thanks, you too, I – Oh, congratulations on the thing.

AIOFE: What?

JASON: Engagement.

LAURA: Jay told me all about it, so – Congrats, you know. It's a – A big fucking step that, but you know – Congrats.

AIOFE: Thank you.

LAURA: Just sorry it had to be with this one cos he's – he's – No, no I'm just joking, I'm just – He's a good one really, he's a good –

AIOFE: I know.

She smiles at JASON.

He smiles.

AIOFE: I'm done chopping the wood, Jase, if you could –

JASON: I'll bring it in.

AIOFE: There's a couple of gas canisters round the back, can you bring 'em in for the kitchen?

JASON: Sure. I'll just – *(Looking at LAURA.)* I –

LAURA: Nah, nah y'alright, you – You –

JASON: Back in a sec.

JASON exits.

LAURA: ...

AIOFE: ...

LAURA: So how you two meet?

AIOFE: Work.

LAURA: You work together?

AIOFE: Yeah.

LAURA: Right, right.

He's great.

AIOFE: I know.

LAURA: I mean, I mean it, he's the fucking –

AIOFE: I know. I'm very lucky.

LAURA: Like, he's a sweetie, he'd like – do anything for you.

AIOFE: Yeah.

LAURA: I mean, like – That's the secret of a successful marriage, innit? Doing anything for each other.

AIOFE: Sacrifice.

LAURA: Sacri – Exactly, exactly that's the – That's the key, innit? Like, doing anything for that other person.

AIOFE: I think you're right.

LAURA: Yeah, yeah it's –

...

AIOFE: ...

LAURA: So, you're Scottish, yeah?

AIOFE: Yeah. Yeah, I am.

LAURA: Cool. Cool. Yeah, I – er – I ain't never been to Scotland before.

AIOFE: No?

LAURA: But I hear it's wicked.

AIOFE: Well – I hope you like it.

LAURA: ...

Right. Yeah.

AIOFE: Your brother's told me a lot about you.

LAURA: Right. All good stuff, I hope.

AIOFE: Yeah. Yeah.

LAURA: Good. That's good.

AIOFE: It's really good to meet you, Laura. I mean that.

LAURA: Right.

AIOFE: Really good.

LAURA: Yeah. Yeah, thanks. You too, I –

AIOFE: I'm glad we can help you.

LAURA: Okay.

AIOFE: We were just gonna get started on some dinner.

LAURA: Oh right.

AIOFE: Would you like to –

LAURA: No, no y'alright, I – I think I'm just gonna – I'm just gonna head off.

AIOFE: What?

LAURA: I gotta –

AIOFE: Laura.

LAURA: Been in your hair and that long enough, I –

JASON enters.

LAURA: Jay, man.

AIOFE: Jason.

JASON: Laura.

LAURA: Jase, I'm gonna – head off, yeah? I'm gonna –

JASON: Law, I –

AIOFE: Did you tell her?

LAURA: Thanks for letting me crash and that, I –

JASON: Law, why don't you sit down?

LAURA: No, no y'alright, I think I'll just –

JASON: Law, just –

LAURA: Let me just get freshened up and a cab and –

JASON: Law.

LAURA: You got a bathroom?

AIOFE: Did you tell her?

JASON: I haven't had the chance yet.

LAURA: Could you pass my bag?

AIOFE: Jason.

JASON: Aiofe, I –

LAURA: Jay?

AIOFE: You need to tell her.

JASON: I know.

AIOFE: You need –

LAURA: Jay, Jay, man can you – Could you pass my bag, I just –

JASON: Laura, why don't you –

LAURA: No, Jase, yeah, Can you – Can you just pass my bag, yeah, I need to – freshen up and then I –

JASON: There's nothing in there.

LAURA: Call a cab and – What?

JASON: I flushed it.

LAURA: What – What you mean?

JASON: I flushed it.

LAURA: ...

What? What you mean – What? I don't –

JASON: The pills and the coke. Little baggy of – Tore it up and I flushed it.

LAURA: ...

   What –

   What you –

   What?

JASON: Law, would you sit down?

LAURA: No, sorry – What –

JASON: Would you –

LAURA: No, what – What the fuck you going through my bag for, Jase?

JASON: Law.

LAURA: What the fuck –

AIOFE: Laura, would you sit down, please?

LAURA: What the fuck?

AIOFE: Would you please –

LAURA: No, no, what yeah, what – What the fuck are you doing going through my –

JASON: Laura.

LAURA: What the fuck –

AIOFE: Laura, you don't need to shout.

LAURA: What the fuck are you doing –

AIOFE: We're not –

LAURA: No, no – It's fine, yeah? It's fine, it – It's fine, yeah, I –

JASON: Laura, we –

LAURA: I'm just gonna call –

JASON: Would you sit down?

LAURA: Where's my phone?

AIOFE: Laura, would you please –

LAURA: Listen, Ee – Ee – Eve, whatever the fuck your fucking name is, I – I just – I know you're tryna be nice and that, yeah? I know you're tryna be nice and that but – But if you just get out of my fucking face, yeah? If you could just get out of my fucking face, yeah, before I – Then that would all be better for us, yeah? That would all – If you could just get out of my fucking face and tell me where my fucking phone is, yeah, then I –

JASON: You didn't have it.

LAURA: What?

AIOFE: When you were at ours last night.

JASON: You said someone took it.

AIOFE: Some guy, he –

LAURA: Okay, fine – Fine you just – I'll just walk and – and find a fucking taxi, yeah, I –

JASON: Laura.

LAURA: I'll just walk.

JASON: Law.

LAURA: Jason would you just fucking leave it, yeah? Would you just – I'm gonna walk and find a – a cab or summat so just tell me where the fuck I –

JASON: There aren't any cabs.

LAURA: What d'you mean there's not any fucking cabs?

JASON: There's not –

LAURA: Course there's a fucking cab, it's not – This is not –

AIOFE: There's no cabs, Laura. Or trains either.

LAURA: What?

AIOFE: Or anything for about twenty five miles. Not till the mainland at least.

LAURA: The fuck are you talking about, you fucking –

AIOFE: So I think we best –

LAURA: What are you talking about? What the fuck are you talking about? What are you –

JASON: Laura.

LAURA: What – I mean, what –

AIOFE: Laura.

LAURA: Where am I? Where the fuck –

JASON: Skaw.

LAURA: What?

JASON: Skaw.

LAURA: What the fuck's Skaw?

AIOFE: North Scotland. Shetland Islands, if you wanna be –

LAURA: ...

What the fuck am I doing in – in –

What the fuck am I doing –

AIOFE: We drove you here. Last night.

LAURA: What – What –

JASON: We put you in the car and we drove you here. All night. Took the ferry over and –

LAURA: What the fuck you do that for? What –

JASON: We're drying you out, Laura.

LAURA: What?

JASON: I'm drying you out.

You turn up on my doorstep last night – our doorstep – You turn up on our doorstep after I haven't seen you in – Covered in vomit and gurning like a – You had a nosebleed so bad I thought you were gonna bleed to death, you – Your blood's so thin from all the – it just – I had to change your clothes, yeah, because you'd pissed yourself. I'm sitting there, scrubbing you in the bath – Aiofe's helping me, she's helping me, she's – I got blood running down my chin from where you – hit it me in the face, split my lip and – Running my tongue over the chipped tooth where I – And I'm thinking all the times I helped you out, yeah? All the times I bailed you out or loaned you money or changed your piss stained clothes and all the years Mum and Dad spent doing it and how they aren't talking to you anymore, they're not – And I keep thinking I should do the same, I should do the same, I should just –

But I can't, Laura. I can't. I can't, I just –

AIOFE: My grandfather had a place – This place – And we thought – Miles away from the – And we thought we'd bring you up here. Get you clean, you know. Help you.

LAURA: Help me?

AIOFE: Yeah.

LAURA: You wanna fucking help me?

AIOFE: We want to help you.

LAURA: Was this your idea, yeah? Was this your –

(To JASON.) Was this her fucking –

JASON: Law.

LAURA: Was this her fucking –

AIOFE: Laura, I am not –

LAURA: *(To AIOFE.)* You fucking –

JASON: Laura, don't –

LAURA: I will eat you, yeah? I will fucking eat you if you don't –

JASON: Laura, don't talk to her like that.

AIOFE: Laura.

LAURA: I will eat you, you stupid fucking cunt, if you don't –

JASON: Don't talk to her like that.

LAURA: I'll talk to her however I fucking well want, I will
fucking –

AIOFE: I'm not scared of you.

LAURA: What?

AIOFE: You can shout at me all you want, Laura. You can shout
and scream at me, it's okay, I'm not –

LAURA tries to attack AIOFE.

AIOFE dodges her.

JASON tries to grab LAURA.

*She turns round and attacks him – shouts and kicks and bites and
screams like a wild animal.*

JASON tries to push her off.

AIOFE grabs LAURA's hand and puts her in a handlock.

LAURA screams in pain and gets off JASON.

AIOFE pins her down on the sofa.

LAURA screams and flails.

JASON holds her other arm.

LAURA: Ah!

JASON: Laura.

LAURA: You fucking –

JASON: Calm down.

LAURA: You fucking –

JASON: Calm down!

LAURA: You fucking –

JASON: If you don't calm down we won't let go of your hands. Do you want us to let go of your hands?

LAURA: You –

JASON: Do you want us to let go of your hands?

LAURA: ...

JASON: Are you going to calm down?

Are you going to calm down?

LAURA nods.

JASON: Are you going to sit down and listen? Are you?

She nods.

JASON: Okay.

They slowly let go of her.

JASON signals for her to sit.

She looks at him.

JASON: Sit down.

She looks at him.

JASON: Sit.

AIOFE: Laura. Please. Sit down.

LAURA: You can't fucking do this.

JASON: You don't leave me much choice.

LAURA: You can't –

JASON: We're doing this, Laura. So help me God, we are fucking doing this.

LAURA: ...

JASON: ...

AIOFE reaches out and gently takes his hand. He softens.

JASON: Just sit down. Please.

He offers LAURA a seat.

She sits.

JASON: Have – Have some water. You're dehydrated. Laura. Have some water. Laura. Have some water.

He offers it to her. She takes it.

AIOFE: I'm going to get started on dinner. We're having lasagne. Is that alright? There's a bit of salad too, some greens, we – Case you haven't got much of an appetite. Why don't you go and wash before dinner?

End.

PLAY 19

PLAY 19 – *Bald Man in a Boat* was first performed at Hackney
Showroom in June 2016, as part of PLAY's *1st Birthday Edition.*
It was later revived at the Edinburgh Festival Fringe for *PLAY
Around,* as part of Paines Plough's Roundabout Season, in
August 2016.

WRITER

Matilda Ibini

Muscavado (Alfred Fagon Audience Award 2015), short plays
at the National Theatre, St James Theatre, Hampstead
Theatre, Royal Exchange Manchester, Birmingham Rep,
Hackney Showroom, Vaults Festival, Bunker Theatre and
Arcola Theatre. Matilda was awarded a scholarship from
BAFTA and Warner Brothers to study an MA in Playwriting &
Screenwriting at City University and studied English Literature
and Creative Writing at London Metropolitan University. She
was part of the Royal Court Writers Program, is a member of
Soho Theatre's Writers' Alumni Group and is part of Tamasha
Playwrights Collective (Year 3). She was also Soho Theatre's
writer-in-residence for the BBC Writersroom 10 scheme. She
is currently Graeae Theatre's artist-in-residence.

DIRECTOR

Holly Race-Roughan

Best Served Cold (VAULT Festival), *Clickbait* and *A First World
Problem* (Theatre 503), *Animal* (Gate Theatre), *Eye of a Needle*
(Southwark Playhouse), and *If Nobody Else Does I Will* (Royal
Exchange).

As associate director: *People Places and Things* (West End/
UK Tour). Holly trained on the Theatre Directing MFA
at Birkbeck College and was resident assistant director at the
Royal Shakespeare Company and Royal Exchange. She is the
Associate Director of the prison arts charity KESTREL.

CAST

Eddie Arnold

Eddie trained at Drama Studio London. Theatre includes: *Life According to Saki* (C Venues), *Hamlet* (Barbican), *The Vote* (Donmar Warehouse), and *Jumpy* (Royal Court/ATG). Television includes: *People Just Do Nothing* (BBC/Rough Cut) and *De Infiltrant* (Eyeworks/Warner Bros).

Isabella Laughland

Theatre includes *BU21* (Trafalgar Studios), *A Further Education* (Hampstead Theatre), *Pride and Prejudice* (Sheffield Crucible), *King Lear* (Chichester/BAM), *The Same Deep Water As Me* (Donmar Warehouse), *The Last of the Haussmans* and *Greenland* (NT), and *Wanderlust* (Royal Court).

Television includes: *Coaches* (Sky), *Lewis* (ITV), and *Black Mirror* (Channel Four).

CHARACTERS

EDDIE, *male*

IZZY, *female*

'…' *indicates words that want to be said but can't be.*

'–' *indicates a break in thought as a new thought overcomes the previous one or an interruption.*

THE INTERVIEW

Lights up.

EDDIE and IZZY are sat next to each other.

A projected screen behind them reads:

    This **was** a couple. You can ask them *anything* you want'

Guidelines for EDDIE and IZZY.

To the audience the situation is real.

Your names are EDDIE and IZZY.

You were a couple with a genuine shared history and memories.

You have been asked to be interviewed on stage for PLAY 19.

You are going to have sex later; you have not had sex since you broke up.

If you are asked whether you would get back together, you have to say <u>no</u>. Even if actually you would.

If you are asked whether you have a partner now you have to say <u>no</u>.

In case no one asks a question – we will ask you a variety of the following.

1. *Why did you break up?*
2. *When did you break up?*
3. *Who broke up with whom?*
4. *How long were you together?*
5. *Who saw whom first?*
6. *When or where did you first have sex?*
7. *What do you both work as?*
8. *Did you use contraception?*
9. *What was your sex life like?*
10. *Have either of you ever cheated?*

11. *Eddie tells us something that Izzy doesn't know.*
12. *Izzy tell us something Eddie doesn't know.*
13. *How many people have you slept with since you broke up?*
14. *Is porn a part of your sex life?*
15. *Are either of you now in a relationship?*
16. *When were you happy together?*
17. *Where did you first meet?*
18. *Would you consider getting back together?*
19. *Were you in love?*
20. *What was the worst night in your relationship?*
21. *Do you have any regrets?*
22. *Have you slept together since?*
23. *Was there ever a pregnancy scare?*
24. *Who's kinkier in bed?*
25. *Who said I love you first?*
26. *Do you still love him or her?*
27. *How serious was the relationship?*
28. *Did you have sex regularly and was it good?*
29. *What's the most annoying thing about him / her?*
30. *Did you meet each other's parents?*
31. *Did you have anal sex?*
32. *Did you ever have a threesome?*
33. *Have either of you ever had an STI?*
34. *When were you proudest of him / her?*
35. *What was your favourite holiday together?*
36. *Who cooks?*

The Q&A should come to a natural conclusion around 5 – 7 minutes.

PLEASURE ZONE

The following scene, movements are accompanied by humming made by IZZY and EDDIE.

Deep intense pink lights.

EDDIE has morphed into a penis.

IZZY has morphed into a clit.

The six steps to climaxing.

1. *Flirting and excitement but they don't touch each other.*

2. *Penis tries to get on top of clit into three different positions and finally finds the right position, before he knows it, he cums!*

3. *Clit is unhappy and jumps out of the penis's arms and shakes off cum.*

4. *Penis is drunk and running around room trying to gear himself up, clit is in the corner clicking, shouting for him to come over and resume.*

5. *Penis gives up and falls to sleep.*

6. *Clit is annoyed and begins to touch herself while looking over to see if penis is watching. She climaxes.*

Blackout.

AFTERPLAY

Penis turns into EDDIE.

Clit turns into IZZY.

In total darkness. Each actor holds a microphone.

EDDIE: Hey. Dude. Dude.

IZZY: Please don't call me dude. This is weird.

EDDIE: Course it's fucking weird.

IZZY: It's just weird being back here in your room and everything is exactly the same. I'm lying in this space that used to be my space. This is so fucking weird.

EDDIE: … I've got a guitar over there. Been taking lessons…so actually it's a bit different… That was fucking nice?

IZZY: Yeah nice one.

EDDIE: Not nice?

IZZY: No, yeah it was nice.

EDDIE: Now it seems like a shit word to use…nice. Like you're a *nice* person. My Grandma's fucking nice. That's basically saying you're pretty – shit. That's the equivalent.

IZZY: You can't make me cum.

EDDIE: I can.

IZZY: You were down there for like five seconds.

EDDIE: It's been fucking three months. Three…

IZZY: – are you saying you don't like my vagina?

EDDIE: No. I do like your vagina – I love your vagina –

IZZY: – so you only go down on girls you're in love with?

EDDIE: No. I'll go down on you now if you want?

IZZY: No.

EDDIE: … I'm sure we've had sex where I didn't go down on you.

IZZY: – yeah well –

EDDIE: – this isn't about –

IZZY: – carry on, carry on –

EDDIE: – It's about what's happened right now –	IZZY: – it's a thing I'm trying to learn from my therapist not to talk over people.

EDDIE: Since when have you been seeing a therapist?

IZZY: In the last year.

EDDIE: Fuck. For what?

IZZY: For stuff.

EDDIE: Like what? You've never –

IZZY: – stuff I don't want to tell you about it's not particularly important.

EDDIE: …

IZZY: I'm not going to tell you now am I –	EDDIE: Are you alright? What's wrong?

IZZY: I don't know what's wrong with me, that's why I'm seeing a therapist.

EDDIE: You can't bring it up then not tell me.

IZZY: It's not important.

EDDIE: Y si te pregunto en español? Como lo hacíamos antes. Cuando estábamos juntos.

(Talk to me. Like we used to. Like we could for hours.)

IZZY: Don't do that. 'Cos you know when you do that…it's really not fair…

EDDIE: Si me acuerdo. Por eso lo estoy haciendo. Cuéntame.

(I know. I remember. That's why I'm doing it. Talk to me.)

IZZY: No – no – no – no – no… I'm getting an Uber.

EDDIE: No quiero que te vayas.

(No. No. No. I don't want you to leave.)

IZZY groans in frustration.

EDDIE: Quédate. Por favor. Si?

(Stay. Please. Yes?)

IZZY: Siiiiiiii… Noooooooooooo.

EDDIE: Podemos empezar de nuevo.

(We can start again.)

EDDIE moves towards IZZY they almost kiss.

IZZY: When I masterbate I cum.

EDDIE is knocked back by the news.

EDDIE: Sorry.

IZZY: When I masterbate I cum.

EDDIE: That's nice.

IZZY: How was sex for you when we were together?

EDDIE: I loved it. I loved having sex with you.

IZZY: I bet you did.

EDDIE: And you didn't?

IZZY: … I loved it…but… I…never orgasmed…

EDDIE: That can't be – what about the time – '

IZZY: – nope.

EDDIE: When we went on holiday –

IZZY: – no.

EDDIE: So what you just faked it?

IZZY: *(Looks down at her feet.)* Yeah… No, I came once…when we watched porn.

EDDIE: Then why would you want to have sex with me again?

IZZY: …

EDDIE: You must have liked it.

IZZY: Yes. I did.

EDDIE: You like having sex with me.

IZZY: Yes – yes. I did like having sex with you.

EDDIE: Then why did you –

IZZY: – I tried to pretend it wasn't a big thing. It's kind of a big thing.

EDDIE: Why didn't you tell me before?

IZZY: Because I didn't know how you'd react. Thought you'd be angry and you were in between jobs. I didn't want to add any more stress.

EDDIE: Fuck… Well what was the point of telling me now? How's that – just fucking made me feel shit.

IZZY: Because if this is something –

EDDIE: – just fucking chuck shit on me.

IZZY: Sorry chuck what –

EDDIE: – so you were just lying?

IZZY: – do you want me to be   EDDIE: I thought we were
    honest?   having great sex.

IZZY: I'm trying. I'm trying to be honest with you. And now
you're saying I'm chucking shit on you?

EDDIE: You're the one giving me the fucking ultimatum. Oh
if you want to get back together you better be making me
cum all the time.

IZZY: Have I said that?

EDDIE: Because –

IZZY: – have I said that –

EDDIE: – because other guys make you cum!

IZZY: Have I said that to you?

Pause.

IZZY: This is why I couldn't…yes other people have done that
to me sometimes. But I liked you. I liked being with you. I
liked everything else about you. But yes this one big thing
you cannot do…for me.

EDDIE: Then I'm no good to you.

IZZY: Have I said that? For fuck's sake!…

EDDIE: Then what are you trying to say?

IZZY: Sex sometimes…it's like your things called a blow job, a
job, but you going down on me is optional.

EDDIE: How much do I owe you then?

IZZY: *That's* not fair.

EDDIE: You only want to be with me, if I can make you cum.

IZZY: …Not all the time.

EDDIE: Why'd you think it's not a big deal for me? It's a fucking huge deal.

IZZY: Is it?

EDDIE: Yes! Of course it is. I just wish you'd had said it before. Fucking two years ago.

IZZY: You should have noticed.

EDDIE: How was I supposed to notice since you were fucking faking it all the time?

IZZY: Because you've been with other women before me. Clearly you're doing something wrong if you can't make girls cum – I'm sorry that was mean – that was really mean – I'm really really sorry.

EDDIE: Please don't touch me… I can make girls cum.

IZZY: Oh yeah.

EDDIE: Yeah, all the time. Sometimes I just to have to look at them.

IZZY: Really?

EDDIE: Of course fucking not but you know, sometimes… It's just easier for guys –

IZZY: – I can cum like (*snaps fingers*) that on my own.

EDDIE: Why did you come here then?

IZZY: To fuck you.

EDDIE: But that's what we just did –

IZZY: Yes…but I hoped you'd fuck me too.

PLAY 26

PLAY 26 was first performed at VAULT Festival, as part of PLAY's *Subterranean Season* in January 2017.

WRITER

Miriam Battye

I Started a Fire (shortlisted for the Bruntwood Prize). Miriam has been a part of the Royal Court Young Writers and Invite Only Group. She was part of the first BBC Drama Room cohort in 2016 and she is a writer on attachment at the Bristol Old Vic.

DIRECTOR

Matt Harrison

Matt is an award winning director and theatre maker who trained at East 15 Acting School and with the National Youth Theatre. He was awarded the 2015 Bryan Forbes Bursary under the mentorship of Michael Attenborough CBE.

Matt has created and directed work at venues including the New Diorama, Finborough, Ambassadors and Criterion Theatre's as well as the National Theatre temporary space. His recent credits include productions with Emma Rice and Kneehigh and he is currently developing new work with Olivier nominated writer James Fritz.

CAST

Jessica Clark

Theatre includes: *Rotterdam* (Trafalgar Studios), *Skin A Cat* (The Bunker), *The Here and This and Now* (Drum, Plymouth), *Romeo and Juliet* and *The Secret Garden* (Storyhouse), *Love's Comedy* (Orange Tree Theatre), *Respect* (Birmingham Rep), and *Be My Baby* (Derby Theatre).

Film, TV and radio includes: *Versailles* (Canal+), *Silent Witness* and *Casualty* (BBC), *Broadside* (PBS Television), and *Kindness* (BBC Radio 4).

Emily Stott

Emily trained at Oxford School of Drama. Theatre includes: *Lines in The Sand* (Soho Theatre), *Tuckshop* (Paines Plough Roundabout), *Circa* (Old Red Lion/Theatre De Meervart), *Gifted* (Theatre503), *A Midsummer Night's Dream* (Catford Broadway Theatre), *After Party* (Union Theatre), *Early Doors* (Pleasance/UK tour), *Electric Eden* (Pleasance), *The Selfish Giant* (Arcola), and *Thirteen* (Southwark Playhouse).

CHARACTERS

ALLY

TOSH

ALLY and TOSH.

They are wrapped around each other.

As soon as we join them, they are speaking. Very quickly. Mid energetic conversation.

ALLY: I decide very early on that we're fucking and then it becomes boring.

TOSH: Ponytail.

ALLY: No. That's a whole other – this guy's just jaw

TOSH: Jaw

ALLY: He's like. He's a jaw and everything else is secondary to that, jaw

TOSH: Nice detail

ALLY: Honestly I've never seen someone with such a present – it's not important. The fuck.

TOSH: The revelatory fuck.

ALLY: Yes.

TOSH: Go from the beginning, I want the play by play, romance me with it

ALLY: Right so by then I'm barely flying at half mast, just trying to stay the fuck awake

TOSH: Good / start

ALLY: I'm pretty much marinated by ten. I had to be. It was a vortex of shit chat, prosecco and bodycon

TOSH laughs briefly.

ALLY: Flapjacks of make up. Scents of sandalwood. Fucking. Gender. Everywhere. As though everyone has to remind each other of their diametric genital qualities

TOSH: Diametric?! TRIPLE WORD SCORE

High five.

ALLY: So I'm waiting for the last dregs of reason to evaporate

TOSH: That was beautiful, you're nailing / this

ALLY: like it's sad but I'm only there for the D by this point. Like I'm conceding that at best I might get some D out of it. For the / story.

TOSH: The story, right

ALLY: and I mean I've been bleeding so much recently it's strange to even get round to the concept of being readily available for entry but I do my best

TOSH: Ride that wave

ALLY: and I'm about to give in when He, the only he at the whole shindig who isn't eating someone already suddenly decides I'm the most promising prospect there

TOSH: arguably / true

ALLY: So he comes at me with his best work, I mean this is top tier stuff, he he he whats that word – he *sidles*

TOSH: Duh-duh *(Jaws theme song.)*

ALLY: What?

TOSH: Jaws.

ALLY: Oh. Ha! Good. Anyway it's all very fucking ordinary but all the tit tape is staring at me like I've just taken a a a dump on the floor I'm *that* objectionable, and he says, 'I don't know you, tell me about you'

TOSH: Cleshic move from the shtud

ALLY: D'you ever think it'd be more effective if they just went, 'Like me please? Please?'

TOSH: 'Pretty please with a cock on top please?'

They laugh. Then –

ALLY: He looked at the business end a lot.

Lights fall.

Movement.

Lights up.

They are stationery.

TOSH: I mean I must've been fairly keen because we don't even leave we just doink in some kids room

ALLY: What?

TOSH: Like I get a Polly Pocket or some shit embedded in my thigh

ALLY laughs briefly.

TOSH: And so he's on me

ALLY: Yeah

TOSH: And this man is big he's colossal I mean *I* look like a fucking Polly Pocket in comparison to his wide load

ALLY: Nice

TOSH: Like he got. / Heft.

ALLY: Heft.

They look at each other. Then –

TOSH: And I get that thing after a while

Y'know like when you wake up and you've got a dead arm

ALLY: Oh I hate that

TOSH: Right but like everywhere

ALLY: A Dead Everywhere

TOSH: Yeah it's like turned off off off insane like I can't even feel him go in

ALLY: Wow

TOSH: I am completely inanimate I'm a fucking fleshlight with semi-conscious being attached to it

ALLY: Wow

TOSH: Oh and I forgot to say by this point we're in zero gravity

ALLY: Right

Lights fall.

Lights up.

They are both squirming, groaning, something gross has just been revealed to TOSH.

ALLY: Oh my god I can't even

TOSH: Wait what the fuck was it?

ALLY: A. Cornetto.

TOSH: Fuck. Capital F

ALLY: Chyeah

TOSH: I mean that is dense with Fuck

ALLY: It was. Nought to sixty in

TOSH: You've gone like zero to Therapy in less than three moves

ALLY: Yeah I know

If I think about it too long I want to hide in my clothes.
Like I need to be in a small space with my breasts.

Something I can understand.

They laugh.

A pause.

TOSH: Just sounds like a whole lot of thrush to me.

A brief pause.

Suddenly groaning and squirming again.

Lights fall.

Lights up.

Movement around the space.

TOSH: And then he comes

ALLY: right

TOSH: and he just explodes into a shower of confetti above me

Like pink and yellow bits of confetti and it covers me head to toe

And I suck it all up into my mouth like a hoover and chew it and spit it out and mould the goop into little statues of Russian dictators

ALLY: Ooh a little spitty Putin

TOSH: A little spitty Stalin

A little spitty...

Actually I can't think of any others but like imagine them all lined up and they look Russian.

ALLY laughs. They pat their little imaginary Russian figureheads.

TOSH breaks all their necks. ALLY laughs.

TOSH: This is so much more fun, isn't it?

ALLY: Yes. Than what. I mean everything with you is more fun than generally everything but specifically what.

TOSH: This is so much more fun than actually being entered.

ALLY: Ah you're funny

TOSH: I know it's terrible. *(Mum voice.)* 'You'll never find a man Tosh if you keep describing how sonorous your farts are'

ALLY: Hey I *love* Tosh's fart chart

TOSH: I know it's magical but. As Mum says. The mens don't wants to fucks the girls who's alls about the gas-s

ALLY: Fuck them

TOSH: Or... Don't

ALLY: Exactly. They don't deserve your fanny or your funny or your farts

TOSH: Eyyyyy!

The triple threat

ALLY: Triple F

TOSH: We should just cork me up, make it official

ALLY: Cork you?

TOSH: Just stuff me rayt up mate

She laughs.

ALLY: Sounds like bliss – can we stuff me up too?

TOSH: *(Voice.)* Ooh would you be obliged to undetake some stuffins?

ALLY: Some a-muffin a-stuffin?

They, as though choreographed, open their legs, leg by leg, daintily.

A pause. And then.

They mime stuffing up each other and their own fannies aggressively with any items around them.

TOSH: Rayt up there mayyyyyyte!

ALLY: Mayyyyttee!

Lights fall.

Lights up.

Space.

ALLY: He tasted like omelette.

TOSH looks at ALLY.

ALLY: He –

TOSH: Sorry can we just
Not talk about cock for a minute.
Cock or what's attached to it

–

I just feel like my head's full of willy
All that's ever going in or out is willy
I haven't even seen one in ages and yet I'm still fucking choking on –
Sorry.

ALLY: Oh.

TOSH: Sorry.

I just need to. Disengage.

ALLY: What else should we talk about?

Lights down.

Lights up.

They are in a different position. REALLY LOUD.

ALLY: 'Who's pussy is this? Who's pussy is this?' He kept
   asking over and over

TOSH: classic

ALLY: and I didn't even respond I

TOSH: that's classic

ALLY: I think he just wanted, 'Yours, yours, yours' et cetera but
   I got a bit lost in the uh the philosophy of it

   TOSH laughs.

ALLY: 'cos I wondered in that moment if the twat was mine, or
   his, or no one's – it was the sex's

TOSH: the what now?

ALLY: Yeah anyway that boy didn't give up suddenly like *Noel's
   House Party* down there

TOSH: Oh my god I *loved* that / show

ALLY: he was after that orgasm

TOSH: Still would by the way

ALLY: Oh yeah Noel can get at me

TOSH: Fucking / DEAL

ALLY: DEAL

   They explode laughing.

ALLY: anyway he was after that orgasm like the fucking the
   fucking the fucking / snitch or

TOSH: Snitch?

   They stare at each other.

ALLY: OH MY / GOD!!

MIRIAM BATTYE

TOSH: OH MY GODDDDDDDD!!

Sewing in the sink! ha.

ALLY: GIMME THE FRIEND COINS BITCH

TOSH makes the Mario golden coins sound and ALLY catches them all.

ALLY: / WE ARE SO IN SYNCCC!!!

TOSH: WE ARE SO IN SYNCCC!!!

Lights fall.

Lights up.

TOSH is touching the side of her forehead. ALLY is wrapped around her.

TOSH: What is this what is this?

ALLY: What?

TOSH: On my fod

ALLY climbs round her and investigates.

TOSH: I've grown like an extra bit of head on my head I can't

She touches it.

ALLY: Oh hello

TOSH: Why've I gone and got this? Have you got this?

ALLY: No I can confirm I'm not growing any additional parts

TOSH: Of course you're probably smooth and fucking.
Bumpless all over
Not like me – I'm.
Expanding

ALLY: It's calcification it looks like

TOSH: What? Calcifi-what?

ALLY: Additional.

> Padding.
> Comes from frequent pressure.

TOSH: Must come from all the phone to head contact I've had
> over the past millenium
> This is you, mate
> This is your shit chat
> Your shit chat has contributed to my, padding

ALLY: Happy to be of service to your
> Growth

TOSH: And my phone bill

ALLY: It should really be free to call someone who's in the
> same flat

TOSH: We need some sort of toilet to lounge fucking phone
> season ticket

ALLY: Let's monitor its progress

Maybe you'll grow a hands free kit

> *ALLY is fiddling with it.*

TOSH: No don't scratch it off! You'll kill him

ALLY: Him?

TOSH: I'm gonna call him Danny Dyer

ALLY: Well I love him.

> I'm in love with him.

> *She kisses Danny Dyer.*

TOSH: You have to name things so as to assume control over
> them

> That's why I name my spots

ALLY laughs.

TOSH: Yeah

Edna, Francesca and Miss Helsey Brown

ALLY: Miss Helsey Brown

TOSH: Yes she's refined

She laughs.

TOSH: And my bacne's all called Josh 'cos it was getting ridic

ALLY: Terrible parenting

TOSH: I know but I'm not proud of them. They're not going to uni.

She laughs.

ALLY: Oof that's some gentle comedy.

TOSH: I'm doing well today.

ALLY: What day is today?

TOSH: I dunno. Give a shit. Monday?

Lights fall.

Lights up.

ALLY is looking at herself in the mirror.

TOSH is curled around her foot.

ALLY: What if they ask me if I have a broad range of interests?

TOSH: You don't need interests your poiffect

ALLY: Yeah like I don't know if fried cheese and sitting and cock is a broad enough range of interests –

TOSH: You like making Gary Barlow memes –

ALLY: Shit I always forget the Barlow card –

TOSH: You like leaning –

ALLY: I love a good lean –

TOSH: You like me. I'm interesting –

ALLY: Yeah yes I should just bring you in just present you as my primary interest since you are basically a product of my womb

TOSH: And I am pissing interesting

ALLY: My massive womb o'friendage

She starts to mime being birthed from ALLY's womb (Yes I said that).

She stops.

TOSH: Wait shouldn't I be birthing you too?

A brief pause.

ALLY: How, is that gonna make anatomical sense?

TOSH: 'Cos what we are concerned about right now is anatomical sense.

A brief pause. Considering.

They suddenly start birthing each other, somehow.

TOSH: Don't go

ALLY: Bread needs to be won.

TOSH: We can steal bread. We can Jean ValJean that shit.

ALLY: *(Sings, grandly.)* 24601

TOSH: / 24601

A pause.

ALLY: It's fine I won't get it

TOSH: Good. Don't you fucking dare.

Lights fall.

They throw themselves at each other. Fun.

TOSH suddenly throws herself really hard at ALLY and collapses onto her like a rag doll.

ALLY tries to stand her up but can't.

She places her on the floor on her back and folds up her knees to her chest lovingly.

Lights up.

TOSH is lying on the floor where ALLY has placed her.

ALLY runs to her, panicked.

ALLY: Tosh Tosh Tosh Tosh Tosh

TOSH: No I'm fine I mean I'm doing terribly but I'm fine

ALLY: Oh my god I thought you might've

TOSH: Just something dropped into my head this morning and knocked a few things over

Something dressed like a man it was well it had a bow tie on that's Man in't it maybe a waistcoat I din't catch the fucker

Um

ALLY: Tosh

TOSH: no but I'm basically completely reasonable totally zen fucking ylang ylang
Tell me about you
Tell me about your day your dreams your ph balance
Fill my head with you please

ALLY: Oh god. Oh god my whole skin flushed cold that was

Fuck

She sits.

ALLY: Can you always remain upright please I don't ever want to walk into a room again and see you / like that

TOSH: Don't leave the room then

ALLY: We need fresh fruit and vegetables.

TOSH: Nah. Let's scurvy UP!

ALLY laughs a little. Kisses TOSH on the head a lot of times.

A brief pause.

TOSH: We can fuse. Like some Superhero fucking dual human megatron.

ALLY: What would our powers be?

TOSH: Unbridled awesome. What would our name be?

ALLY: Double Girl.

TOSH: Ah you ruined it.

Lights fall.

Lights up.

A pause.

ALLY: I love you.

TOSH: Good.

A pause.

TOSH: Can we kill everyone else yet?

ALLY: Yep.

Lights fall.

TOSH holds onto ALLY as she tries to move around the space.

Lights up. Standing far apart.

ALLY: All right Single White Female

TOSH: Shuddup You're literally *growing* on me I'm carrying you around with me on my face I

ALLY: Wait I'm not Danny Dyer

TOSH: Fucking SHUT UP I'm SAYING SOMETHING ACTUAL NOW

I'm *sick* of trying to persuade you that I am worth as much time and energy as your boys.

I love you, and my love is worth much more. My love is solid fucking blood diamond compared to his shit ass cruddy shitttttt love.

ALLY: Who are you talking about? There's no –

TOSH: Don't you get it yet?

I am worth *more* because I receive less from you and yet I continue to contribute.

I am keeping you alive. You need to keep me alive.

ALLY holds TOSH by the shoulders.

ALLY: I haven't seen a man in almost a year
At your request
I haven't even
You've

TOSH: What happened in your early life that made you *so* want the shitty version of love that they give you?

ALLY: That's horrible.

TOSH: Yes. It is.

ALLY: What more can I –

TOSH: Just just just

>   Stop being fucking

>   *Casual*

ALLY: I'm not!

TOSH: Can you just dig in please.

>   Can you just hair up pull on your joggers and dig into us.

>   *A brief pause.*

ALLY: Okay.

>   *Lights fall.*

>   *Lights up. TOSH is sitting on ALLY's knee.*

TOSH: It's funny at school we used to sit on girls in the lower years sit right on them hard and make them describe a penis – y'know the ones who swore they weren't fridges – and every time they got a bit anatomically wrong or whatever we'd smack them on the back of a neck with a Shatter resistant ruler did I ever tell you that?

ALLY: Um

TOSH: They nicked a Biology textbook out the science lab and were all passing it round fucking trying to revise before we got to them I still remember them all sweating.

>   *A brief pause. TOSH suddenly isn't laughing.*

TOSH: Am I bad? I've never felt Bad before but I think there a bit of pure Bad in that, isn't it?
I'm sure you don't know.
I'm sure you're too –

ALLY: I stole Martha Frampton's pants out of her gym bag once.

TOSH: What?

ALLY: I didn't know what to do with them so on the way home I stuffed them through a postbox. I don't know why I did it but I remember watching her walk around all day and knowing she didn't have any pants on.

A brief pause.

ALLY: Fucking slut.

Lights fall.

Lights up.

They are moving. Energy.

TOSH: Hoover.

ALLY: I hear you.

TOSH: Hoover. Sofa. Watermelon. Armpit. In that order.

ALLY: Armpit? Felthy betch

TOSH: Nah I'd tie a string around it and puppet it and play with it all day long

ALLY: Get it a teeny tiny moustache and a pair of peen glasses

TOSH: Monacle, mate. Jap's solo eye

She laughs. She does a monacle.

ALLY: Very good

TOSH: Sorry Japs

ALLY: Ten points from Gryffindor for / racial

TOSH: Ravenclaw, mate

ALLY's phone starts ringing.

TOSH: Who's that?

ALLY: Uh. Man again.

I should

TOSH: Nah

ALLY: He's been threatening coming over

TOSH: We'll set up traps

FUCK OFF AND DIE CHODENUGGET

They shoot at the phone DIE DIE DIE etc. ALLY goes to pick it up.
TOSH knocks it out of her hand hard, it shocks ALLY a bit.

TOSH: Let's dance to it

They dance to the ringtone throughout the next. Laughter.

TOSH: You. Okay. What would you do. Go.

ALLY: With what? A peen?

TOSH: Pina colada. Yeah.

A pause. She thinks.

ALLY: I'd train it. To respond. To the music of. Anastasia. On
the recorder.

TOSH: And it would rise to her peanut butter voice like a
charmed snake.

ALLY: Mate you know that voice is. Claggy. As shit.

They laugh.

TOSH: 'I'm outta love, set me free'

ALLY: 'I'm outta love, set me free'

A pause.

ALLY: Actually I reckon I'd chop it off. Roast it. Shallots. Honey & mustard. Bed o' kale.

TOSH: Ooh god my whole mouth just filled with saliva.

ALLY: I'd consume, no chewing. World could do with one less sentient dildo.

Lights fall.

Mad dancing. Brief.

Sudden stop. Lights up.

ALLY: Do you ever worry if we're healthy?

TOSH: No.

ALLY: You don't think about that?

TOSH: I don't worry about it.

Brief pause.

ALLY: If you ever die I'll kill you.

TOSH: If you ever leave me I'll kill you more.

ALLY: I'll eat your skin.

TOSH: I'll eat your heart.

ALLY: I'll chop off your knees.

TOSH: I'll rip off your lips.

ALLY: I'll sharpen your elbows.

TOSH: I'll tie you to a tree.

Set fire to it.

A brief pause.

ALLY: Good.

Lights fall.

Lights up.

They are far apart. A long time has passed.

TOSH: I know it's crazy insane.

ALLY: It's crinsane.

TOSH: Ha – It's like *just* enough to keep me conscious and also, like, *delighted.* All the time. Without legally being high. New neighbours are *top.*

ALLY laughs a little.

ALLY: I thought I could smell it when I came in.

A pause. Itchy.

TOSH: Mate Brexit was shit, wasn't it?

ALLY: Yeah that sucked my b-hole.

Polite laugh.

TOSH: And a moment's silence for our dearly departed friend, Sanity.

Hands on hearts. Maybe ALLY does some sort of Last Post on a fake trumpet.

A pause. Polite laughter.

ALLY: I saw all the camels.

TOSH: Yeah.
    Fucking.
    Trying to be funny.
    Not my idea.

ALLY: Yeah. I thought.

TOSH: Sorry I didn't –

ALLY: Oh god no –

TOSH: We only had –

ALLY: No literally it's completely –

TOSH: Like I don't even know half of –

> *They both descend into awkward sort of half-speaking-polite-hilarious-bullshit.*

> *A pause. Laughter dies.*

TOSH: Isn't it so nice when you can like meet up after like years and it's like exactly the same

ALLY: Yeah it's **great**.

> *A pause.*

ALLY: Is he funny?

TOSH: What?

ALLY: Is he funny?

TOSH: No.

ALLY: Right.

TOSH: But he's –

> *She thinks.*

> *Hard.*

> *A pause.*

TOSH: You know.

ALLY: Yeah. I mean I don't. But. "Yeah".

> *A pause.*

TOSH: So like, how are you? Are you seeing anyone? What are you up to?

ALLY looks at her, seethes.

Lights fall.

PLAY 27

PLAY 27 – *A Brief History of Holding Hands* was first performed at VAULT Festival, as part of PLAY's *Subterranean Season* in March 2017.

WRITER

Jessica Siân

Klippies (nominated for three Offie Awards including Most Promising New Playwright, Southwark Playhouse) and *Kiki's Delivery Service* (Southwark Playhouse). Jessica is an actor and playwright. She is currently under commission at the Bush Theatre. Her work has been supported by the National Theatre Studio, HighTide and Hampstead Theatre and she is a Royal Court Young Writers alumni.

DIRECTOR

John Young

To Dream Again and *Scattered* (Theatre Clwyd), *We Know Where You Live* (Finborough Theatre), *A Place in the Woods* (Tristan Bates Theatre), *The Watchers* (Southwark Playhouse), *What the Walls Saw* and *The Thing Is* (Grosvenor Park Open Air Theatre), and *Soft Beats the Heart* (Theatre503).

John is a former Resident Assistant Director at The Finborough Theatre and prior to this was on the Emerging Trainee Director Scheme at Theatre Clwyd.

CAST

Anita-Joy Uwajeh

Anita-Joy trained at Drama Centre London.

Theatre includes: *Twelfth Night* (Shakespeare's Globe), *Girls* (Hightide/Soho Theatre), *Fury* (Soho Theatre), and *We Wait In Joyful Hope* (Theatre503).

Television includes: *Lucky Man* (Sky1) and *Cut* (Channel 4/ Clerkenwell Films).

Ben Norris

Ben trained at the Royal Welsh College of Music and Drama, he is a writer and actor. Theatre includes: *The Hitchhiker's Guide to the Family* (Underbelly/Southbank Centre).

Television and radio includes: *The Liquid You* (BBC Radio 4) and *Send Her Victorious* (Channel 4).

CHARACTERS

AJ

BEN

AJ is admiring the communal garden

AJ: It's beautiful. I mean it. There was nothing like this when we were kids. I mean it's fucking, wow /

BEN: It's still early /

AJ: Well yeah but it's, I mean it's not even spring, in spring, can you imagine? I mean wow, what you've done is, and in this 'fucking shit-hole', I mean, not, you know what I mean, are these tulips?

BEN: It's been really mild so /

AJ: Yeah, yeah, yeah. Wow. This is just /

BEN: AJ /

AJ: You could expand you know? The kids come down right?

BEN: KS1 up to year 6, they get /

AJ: Yeah, great and the parents?

BEN: Well some of them bring the kids at the weekends but /

AJ: You should get the parents, that's the crux of the fucking problem you know, a whole generation of kids raising… that's what we need to…is it just flowers?

BEN: Well we started with /

AJ: I mean flowers are great, I'm not saying…

BEN: The little ones like flowers, little effort big reward /

AJ: Sure, sure, but I mean, fuck flowers, think big, I get it, I mean I'm sure they love, you know, running around all Jackson Pollock with their fucking poppy seeds but /

BEN: Well I wouldn't say /

AJ: Not, no, I mean, I'm not saying…but, I'm saying, I'm saying vegetables… Right? Am I right? Like teach them to grow you know, turn a seed into a carrot and actually fucking eat it.

BEN: We've got some grow bags coming, garden centre donated so that's /

AJ: Great, yes, I mean that's what I'm saying, you could really expand this, that bit of car park outside the walk-in centre, sitting there, empty, no fucking cars, could use that?

BEN: Well taking up the concrete might be /

AJ: Get planning permission. You could get funding for this, apply to the council, application process's a nightmare but I could help you / with that

BEN: AJ /

AJ: I don't mean, I know about this sort of thing's all I'm / saying

BEN: AJ /

AJ: With the right organisation this could really make a difference /

BEN: Stop. AJ, stop, just stop. Ok?

AJ: I'm just trying to be encouraging.

BEN: Look at me. What was that?

AJ meets BEN's eye for a moment but can't hold his gaze.

AJ: I couldn't face it in there ok, I'm sorry, Shanai with her fucking funeral face on, stuffing it full of sausage rolls, pretending to cry while she counts his cash, chubby cunt.

BEN: Yeah well… Was that a veil she had on?

AJ: Like she's fucking Jackie Kennedy?

BEN: You did go off on one though.

AJ: I wanted one thing right? One thing of my Mums, you know that watch she always, that little gold watch my Mum…

BEN: Yeah

AJ: I said I'd come down, I'd leave right after, no fuss, nothing leave her to it, the house, whatever I just want that watch but no, turn up today says she can't find it.

BEN: Maybe she can't… *(AJ gives BEN a disparaging look.)* Ok, well, do you know where it is?

AJ: I know where I left it.

BEN: You going to the house   AJ: You seeing anyone

   …

BEN: Uh, no.

AJ: I don't have a key.

BEN: Never stopped you before? They'll be at the Horse for hours yet?

AJ: I can't?

BEN: Give you a leg up?

   Laughing

AJ: Fuck I'm unfit

BEN: I really wasn't dressed for that.

AJ: It was your idea.

BEN: Yeah, well, my memory of breaking in through your bedroom window is a little rose tinted I guess.

AJ: Fucking hell, it's…

   It's the same. It's exactly the same.

BEN: Creepy.

AJ: Shit, look at that, I swear I thought I was gonna marry
Usher… I mean Jesus he hasn't even changed the sheets,
it's a shrine.

BEN: Maybe he thought you'd come home.

AJ: She'll be right in now, bet she can't wait to turn it into a…
I don't know, home gym, fat spar, fucking QVC cross-
trainer, as if it makes a difference she's been fat forever,
dieting as long as I've /

BEN: Christ!

AJ: What?

BEN: Was that Halloween or something?

AJ: Tracy Thompson's Spice Girl party.

BEN: Oh shit, yes, didn't some little princess tell you you
weren't allowed to be Sporty Spice?

AJ: Yeah, you going as Ginger though, totally fine, we should
start / looking

BEN: You punched her, said you'd been to Judo and that's as
sporty as it gets…

AJ: I know it's in a box, just, check under the bed would you?

BEN: It's all boxes under here, how were you such a hoarder
and I never noticed?

They hunt.

AJ: God there's so much shit in here, I bet there's like some
statistic, if you did like a study, that we built eighty percent
of todays landfills with tat from the nineties /

BEN: Tampon /

Pulling out a plastic aubergine from one of the boxes.

AJ: I mean what the fuck?

BEN: It was just after your mum died, wasn't it? No wonder you punched her.

AJ: Yeah well, kids are cruel, can you have a go round the other side? Ha, look at this:

AJ pulls out a signed school shirt.

BEN: Is that Ashraf Patel?

AJ: Totally fancied him.

BEN: You did not.

AJ: I did.

BEN: Well feeling must've been mutual he's drawn you a lovely picture of his dick. Fucking hell, there's more boxes this side.

AJ: I'm pretty sure it's a Reebok box.

BEN: Went up to the reservoir after.

AJ: After when?

BEN: Tracy's party.

AJ: Right.

BEN: Said that was our place.

AJ: Maybe it's a Nike box /

BEN: CD, I must've burnt it you, AJ & Ben 4 EVA /

AJ: Fuck, I'm gonna miss my train.

BEN: What?

AJ: I've got a train back at six.

BEN: Right.

AJ: What?

BEN: No, nothing, just…

AJ: I can't just stay here.

BEN: No, you've made that clear.

AJ: Ben?

BEN: Let's just find the fucking watch, ok.

BEN moves to look through a box stage left. AJ sees the CD BEN had discarded, she opens the case, rediscovering it, breaths on it as though fogging up a window, wipes the back gently with her sleeve and puts it on.

Ja Rule's 'Always on Time' (feat. Ashanti) comes on:

They hear the first chords & the memory of their shared history shoots through them like an electric shock.

BEN starts singing along to the song.

BEN starts to really go for it, doing some of Ashanti's moves and riffing over the melody. Then as AJ's part nears he starts to rev her up in between bits of singing.

The following should be over the above verse and before Ja Rule's first bars.

BEN: Come on, you know you want to.

AJ: No way, no way /

BEN: Don't do this to me, I'm serious / don't

AJ: I'm not doing it /

BEN: leave me hanging, come on, come on, come on…

Just as Ja Rule's first line comes in AJ can't help herself and launches into a perfect impression.

She starts to dance right up close to BEN, he's watching her.

They kiss.

AJ starts to untuck BEN's shirt.

BEN pulls away. Throws her off. Removes himself.

AJ slowly wipes BEN's lipstick from her bottom lip…

AJ: Sorry /

BEN: Yup

AJ: I didn't mean to /

BEN: Yeah…

AJ: I didn't…

BEN: Did you mean to leave without a word?

AJ: Ben /

BEN: Did you mean to not call? To not pick up the phone? Fuck… Facebook? Fucking find a friend? Whatever for twelve years?

AJ: I didn't know how to /

BEN: Come on /

AJ: I had to get out of here, I had to get away from that…whale woman you know that /

BEN: You made sure you got away from everyone /

AJ: I just, once I was out there, it just seemed easier to /

BEN: And what? What was that? 'Are you seeing anyone', come down for a little trip down memory lane, little spoonful of nostalgia and then off you go, not even stay the night. What? Were we gonna fuck on your sixth form bed and you'd do a runner /

AJ: No, I, I didn't even know if I was gonna see you and then you were at the funeral and you're doing great and you look great and /

BEN: No thanks to you, I don't need you to 'talk to the council'. Miss, 'voice of the working classes' /

AJ: Jesus, it was just /

BEN: No, you think I don't know what this community needs, you think I need you to tell me how I should be trying to work with the parents and get people involved /

AJ: Oh come on /

BEN: When you just fucked off /

AJ: Yeah, alright then /

BEN: Without a word /

AJ: That's what this is about, that's why I never phoned never fucking Facebooked whatever /

BEN: Why, why, why, because you're ashamed /

AJ: No, because you're jealous and I knew you would be /

BEN: Oh my god /

AJ: Yeah, yeah, I got out, I had the guts to get out /

BEN: Run away / you mean

AJ: Build a life for myself a new life, away from this dump and do well for myself /

BEN: Yeah /

AJ: I'm fucking successful /

BEN: Oh yeah, I saw you on the Wright Stuff, practically Beyonce /

AJ: Fuck off /

BEN: I don't give shit your on telly, I don't give a shit. I know you, I know you're a broken little girl and, and, and a fattist /

AJ: Oh come /

BEN: And I'm proud of what I do here because it's real, it's for real people not for clicks and retweets and fucking /

AJ: You know what Ben, take a look out your fucking window, this place is a shit-hole, it's always been a shit-hole and you're just fucked off the grass is greener where I'm standing /

BEN: The grass is greener where you fucking water it AJ.

AJ: I've got a train to catch /

BEN: Yeah run along.

AJ: I have responsibilities.

BEN: You just buried your father, you've come home for the first time in years and you can't wait to get away, why'd you even bother coming back /

AJ: Guess I wanted to see if there was anything worth coming back for /

BEN: Got your answer have you?

AJ: Yeah, yeah I do.

/

BEN: Dead fox in there.

AJ: Stupid place to come if you didn't want to be found.

BEN: Yeah well...

AJ: You walk up here in those?

BEN: They're Manolo, I carried them. Missed your train.

AJ: That'll be the first time someone's lorded Manolo Blahnik in this dog-end town. Want some of this?

AJ offers him sip from the flask in her coat.

BEN: Stop that /

AJ: I'm just teasing /

BEN: No, if this is a shit-hole then I'm shit, do you get that? If you got out, got away, you got away from me, just fucking stop it.

AJ: It's just…it's just words.

BEN: Sticks and stones is it?

AJ: Yeah /

BEN: Yeah well, they fucking hurt. You have no idea how cynical you are do you?

AJ: I am not. I'm a positive person. I am, I do fucking yoga!

BEN: This place disgusts you, Shanai disgusts you, your father disgusted you, fuck I disgust you /

AJ: That's not /

BEN: And the fact that you still want me, even though I'm still here, haven't done any thing, gone any where, that this place is enough for me, that disgusts you.

…

BEN: Give me that. Am I so horrible /

AJ: No /

BEN: That you couldn't call me, you couldn't come and see me, you just, you just left.

AJ: I wanted to be brand new, I wanted to have never existed before, never, I wanted to have no history, nothing to define me, nothing to tell me who I was or what I was or what I should be or behave like or… I wanted to be new. I wanted to be born again completely new and… I was right,

I come back here for, hours just, not even a day and it's like climbing into the Trainspotting toilet and I'm right in the shit. I'm right back here, with you and It's not true, not everything disgusts me, but this place isn't enough so we just, we never would've made it.

BEN: I teach this little girl, her name's Jenna Taylor, I know, her parent's don't hear it, it's, it's child abuse, but she's obsessed with the sixties, Mary Quant, fucking Sex Pistols, all that, she came to national book day dressed as Viv Albertine, one of The Slits? She's got this book aparently.

AJ: OK.

BEN: She understands something about herself, something potent about who she is based on what was, she's tethered, she has an anchor, she's not just floating, she's real because of what came before. That is something.

AJ: I don't want to be tethered. I want to move forward, no looking back, no turning to salt. I need everything to be new.

BEN: Are you seeing anyone?

AJ: It's not serious /

BEN: Fucking hell /

AJ: I'm sorry.

BEN: You're killing me here. I was at the station the day you went, I read your diary, you'd been being fucking weird and I knew something was up /

AJ: Wow.

BEN: Yeah well, I waited for weeks for you to tell me what you had planned, ask me to come with you, to run away together. I stood on the bridge looking over the platform, what was it, first train, like five AM? Waiting for you to look up, I knew that if you looked up you wouldn't be able to go, you'd see me and you'd know that you couldn't be whole without me and you'd never get on that train. And the train pulled in, and you stepped on and you left and all this time I've been asking myself why you never looked up and I should have been wondering why the fuck I didn't shout, run down onto the platform, get on the train with you. I wanted it to be magic. And now we're up here, 'our place', first place we kissed, first place we got stoned, first place we...and I still do.

AJ: I don't believe in magic.

BEN pulls the small gold watch from his jacket pocket.

BEN: Adidas box.

AJ: Come with me now?

BEN: Come back?

AJ takes BEN's hand.

AJ: I can't.

    ...

BEN: They've finished the sausage rolls by now.

AJ: Fatty finished 'em hours ago, Dyson on a plate of finger sandwiches. It's almost pretty from up here.

BEN: Yeah, almost.

Lights.

PLAY 29

PLAY 29 was first performed at VAULT Festival, as part of PLAY's *Subterranean Season* in March 2017.

WRITER

Samuel E. Taylor

CANIS and *solo[solo]* (Theatre West at Bristol Old Vic). Samuel was writer on attachment with Bristol Old Vic via the Creative England iWrite and BBC Writersroom 10 schemes, he is a graduate of the Royal Court Young Writers Programme. His first feature film *Benbecula* is in development with Wellington Films.

DIRECTOR

Jocelyn Cox

Ménage a Moi (Bunker Theatre), *Star Jelly* (Royal Exchange Theatre), *The Baby Act* (Barbican/RichMix), *Black Bodies* (Royal Exchange Theatre), and *On A Quiet Street in Bolton* (Octagon Theatre).

As assistant director: *1984* (Playhouse Theatre), *Uncle Vanya* (Almeida Theatre), *The Ancient Secret of Youth and the Five Tibetans* (Octagon Theatre), and *Private Lives* by Noel Coward (Octagon Theatre).

Jocelyn was a Resident Director at the Almeida Theatre and in residence as Assistant Director at Octagon Theatre, Bolton supported by RTYDS.

CAST

Richard Leeming

Richard trained at the Oxford School of Drama.

Theatre includes: *Dr Faustus*, *Don Quixote* and *The Alchemist* (RSC) and *A Midsummer Night's Dream* (Squerryes Court). Television includes: *Doctors* and *Shakespeare Live* (BBC).

David Palmstrom

David trained at Drama Centre. Theatre includes: *A Midsummer Night's Dream* (Lewes Castle), *Tender Napalm* (Mosaic Festival), *Treasure* (Finborough Theatre), *The Ruby in the Smoke* (Brighton Fringe) and *5 Guys Chillin'* (King's Head).

NOTES

In the original performance David and Richard wore
identical costume and were barefoot. They also wore
wireless headset microphones in the tradition of TED.
Silicon Valley Lifestyle Guru was the intended look.

The text is designed for two performers.

A line break indicates a change in speaker.

When one performer is not speaking, he/she should be
performing a section from the High Intensity Interval
Training routine detailed throughout.

This routine should gradually increase in intensity
mirroring the crescendo reached in the spoken text.

The whole thing should be a matter of endurance. Aim
to be sweating buckets and gasping for air by the end.

Good evening.   *[neck rolls]*

Thank you to TED for inviting me to share
with you all.

I hope what I have to say will be of some
value.

_____

You probably recognise me from movies   *[leg stretches]*
such as *X-Men: Days of Future Past, Assassin's
Creed, 12 Years a Slave,* the blockbuster *300,*
with Gerard Butler.

If none of those ring any bells, some of you
might recall, early on in my career, way
back in 2002, I played a character called
Christian Connolly in an episode of *Holby
City.*

_____

As you might imagine my line of work   *[arm stretches]*
means I spend a lot of time in trailers, or in
lengthy hotel press junkets or in airport VIP
lounges.

When I was asked to do this talk, I won't lie
I had second thoughts.

I did my best to try and think of specific
instances that might begin to illuminate for
you the sorts of feelings that start to swallow
me when I have to spend extended periods
of time on my own.

But the truth is I can't begin to describe how
it feels.

I just can't.

The story I am able to tell you begins when I was working on the 2013 crime-thriller *The Counsellor*. *The Counsellor* is an ensemble piece. Other than *yours truly* the headline cast included Penelope Cruz, Brad Pitt, Javier Bardem, Cameron Diaz…quite a line up you'd have to agree.

[dynamic arms – a sort of windmill gesture, one side, then the other, then both]

The shoot itself was dogged by problems from the beginning. Firstly, and this was a view shared by the majority of the crew, the script was total manure. Even Cormac McCarthy, the writer, said so.

It is my strong belief that the producers raised the cash for the movie purely based on the strength of the cast, and hoped that might be enough to gain decent returns at the box office.

This turned out not to be the case.

It's the first day of principle photography and my PA Susan Jimenez Castro has been stricken down with tonsillitis.

[elephant trunk arm figure of eight]

I'm left to fend for myself. I manage well enough for the first few hours but by lunchtime, I'm desperate. I've run out of Guava and catering don't have any green tea.

The producers have arranged a new assistant but she's coming all the way from

Juarez. We're way out in the Yucatan
Peninsula.

It's possible I'll have to manage by myself
for days.

I've heard rumours about a minimart on the   *[lunges]*
freeway a few miles west.

Leonard from make-up tells me Javier
Bardem made his PA travel there on
foot to secure him a less corrosive brand
of chap stick. The ease with which my
colleague Bardem is so apparently cruel
to his subordinates makes me question his
judgement, but I nonetheless find myself
sympathising with him.

The desert makes monsters of us all.

Until my new PA arrives I have no choice.   *[leg swings]*
I certainly can't last much longer in this
damned Mexican heat without a suitably
pro-immune pick-me-up.

I leave the comfort of my trailer and make
my way out into the wilderness.

I'm walking for literally an hour or so   *[mountain*
before I spot the minimart, glistening on the   *climbers]*
horizon.

I allow myself a deep sigh of relief.

But for a moment I forget the reality of my situation.

Get a grip, I whisper to myself.

Your desire for fresh fruit and anti-oxidants is nothing compared to the cravings Provisional Irish Republican Bobby Sands must've endured during his struggle against a particularly savage British Government, an endurance which you portrayed (to critical acclaim) in the 2008 drama, *Hunger*.

It's a relief to be inside the minimart. The air conditioning is cool.

[mountain climber star jumps]

I take out my shopping list.

A ripe Guava.

Green, White, Cabbage or Thistle Tea.

Broccoli Butter and the freshest swordfish I can lay my Irish hands on.

I've done three laps of the store before I realise there is zero chance of purchasing anything from my list in this hovel.

Distraught, I slump into a heap by the checkout when I hear a kindly sounding voice say my name.

Mr Fassbender?

I look up.

[press-ups]

A young man is standing in front of me.
A handsome strapping type. He looks
concerned to see me in my current state.

Yes?

Are you okay?

I can't bring myself to answer the
benevolent stranger's question.

He extends a hand and helps me to my feet.

Outside the minimart my new acquaintance
George produces an ice cold fennel cordial
from his cooli bag and we share it.

[sit-ups]

Fennel, coincidentally, is my favourite of the
perennial herbs.

It is remarkably well suited for juicing.

I tell George a little about my weekly
cleansing routine. From the way he's
looking at me I get the feeling he would like
to hear more but I remember I promised
Ridley Scott I'd be back in my trailer before
sundown.

I go to shake George's hand when he pulls
me in close.

We're face to face.

George looks me straight in the eyes with
an intensity I haven't seen since my days on
set with Viggo Mortensen rehearsing for the
movie *A Dangerous Method*.

George tells me quite matter of fact-ly that he is my biggest fan.

I'm your biggest fan, Michael.

I smile.

If I'm honest, by this point I've become desensitised to this particular combination of words.

Let it be noted that to my infinite shame I failed to recognise the honesty in George's voice.

———————————————

Six weeks later and the shoot is finished.

[bleep test 2 – fast]

I can't bring myself to speak to anyone at the wrap party.

Everyone looks so pleased with themselves.

Penelope Cruz has set up a face-painting booth, Bardem is gorging himself on fondue, Cameron Diaz is explaining the plot of *Charlie's Angels: Full Throttle* to my stuntman, Lachlan Atlantis.

But what do they all have to be so happy about? I feel sick when I realise that in the middle of all this frivolity I am isolated.

I am utterly alone.

The barman is sorting me another Campari and white wine when I realise the man who's been pouring me this delicious drink all evening (a drink which the bartender

SAMUEL E. TAYLOR

instinctually guessed was my tipple of
choice) is none other

than my minimart compadre and Superfan,
George.

Despite knowing next to nothing about the
young gent I am filled with a warm feeling
at the sight of him.

He asks how the shoot went. I joke, telling
him he'll have to buy a ticket and see the
damn thing.

We both laugh.

I'm glad to see George. Right now he's my
one true friend in this nauseating tavern of
sycophants.

I'm not sure what comes over me but I lean
across the bar and take him by the lapels.

*Would you come with me, George? To London,
England?*

George doesn't say anything. He just grins.

George agrees to come with me on one
condition… That I teach him everything I
know about becoming what he describes as
Übermensch.

*[knees high,
heels high –
alternating]*

My ancestral German tongue means I
understand that Übermensch translates
roughly as *ultimate man* or *super-man*.

George says something but it's loud in the bar and I don't hear him.

[star jumps, press-ups, knees to palms, jogging on the spot]

Though later, on the flight from Acapulco International to Heathrow I'm half asleep when George leans over and mutters into my ear, *I meant you, Michael.*

I want to be like you.

_____

George is keen to begin learning as soon as possible.

We've started simple with some high intensity interval training but our relationship quickly transcends the physical.

[apply a cleansing facial mask]

George is not your average humble bumpkin and I am not your typical role model.

Beauty. Wellness. Strength. Stamina.

I teach George it all.

I am his master.

His sensei.

He is my Padawan.

_____

George keeps me company. He nourishes my soul whilst in turn I improve his general aesthetic and approach to life.

[extreme skipping]

George tells me he used to exercise a little in his garage back home.

But together we take things to the next level.

Not only is George beginning to shed all the excess baggage he's nurtured over the years (emotionally and literally).

[remove cleansing facial mask]

he's also developing a keen interest in the physiology involved in maintaining a winning mental attitude such as mine.

I tell him everything he wants to know, and he wants to know everything.

How is my jawline so well defined?

Is there a chemical secret behind that twinkle in my eye?

How do I concentrate on achieving my goals?

Why does everyone I meet instantly like me?

When do you know it's time to stop?

The truth is I never stop.

Never.

I tell him if I stop then I'll realise I'm all by myself.

We share a moment together.

George puts his hand on my shoulder.

[burpees]

George puts his hand on my cheek.	*[burpees]*
————————————	
George puts his hand on my knee.	*[burpees]*
————————————	
You're not alone anymore, Michael.	*[burpees]*
————————————	
George is amazing. We spend a lot of time together.	*[burpees]*
————————————	
George is exciting. We spend all our time together.	*[burpees]*
————————————	
George is beautiful and fun and we spend every waking minute together.	*[burpees]*
————————————	
It feels like I've known George for weeks (which I have).	*[burpees]*
————————————	
We've not been that social since returning to London so we decide to treat ourselves to a night out, but word soon gets out that I'm back in town.	*[mix large protein shake and consume]*

Friday. Boys night. Ronnie Scotts.

Me, George, my onscreen foe and occasional friend James McAvoy, James Franco, James Norton, James Cordon, James

Nesbitt, James Earl Jones, Alex James and Drake.

It's a relaxed affair, a few White Russians among friends, but soon enough filth merchant McAvoy is cranking the dial up to eleven.

Having spent a good half an hour rudely ignoring the group (developing a secret handshake with boy's night rookie James Earl Jones) McAvoy demands the house band give our booth a shout out which he insists (upon threat of cancellation of his quite considerable monthly membership fee) be henceforth known as *cosy corner.*

When he doesn't return from a toilet break it becomes clear that McAvoy is out of control. Nesbitt informs the group that McAvoy is refusing to leave the restroom until the attendant, who proffers a variety of cologne, say the words *no Armani, no punani*

George, ever the smart and considerate cookie, is worried about the debauchery getting leaked to the press. He clocks a fire exit, throws his fine burgundy knit over my head and escorts me from the premises. Drake, aware of how damaging shenanigans like this can be to one's personal brand, follows suit.

It's a relief to get away.

[bleep test 1 – medium]

In the taxi George is kind and caring as always. He checks I'm okay, hands me a bag of seaweed thins, and tells me to pull myself together.

Drake finds George funny.   *[punch jump]*

Drake sniggers like a little girl.   *[punch jump]*

Drake sniggers like a coward.   *[punch jump]*

Drake sniggers like a little bitch.   *[punch jump]*

George shoots Drake a look, but lets it go. *[sidewinders]*

I'm having mixed emotions. The night is collapsing in on me.

I feel bad for leaving the James's back at the club.

I'm feeling faint.

George takes out his cooli bag and fixes two protein shakes.

One for him, one for me.

George likes to do whatever I do.

Drake doesn't understand.

How could he?

How could anyone?

He flips.

He uses language which upsets George.

George shoots Drake another look.

George shoots Drake another look and asks him to be quiet.   *[superman + sit-up]*

George tells Drake to be quiet.   *[burpees]*

George puts Drake in his place   *[sit-up]*

George swears at Drake, putting him in his place.   *[press-up]*

George swears and screams at Drake.   *[core paddle]*

George swears and screams and spits at Drake.   *[bleep test 3 – sprints]*

George tells the driver to pull over.

George kicks the taxi door open and gestures for Drake to get out.   *[burpees]*

George makes Drake get out of the taxi.

In the middle of nowhere.

In Bethnal Green.

Drake doesn't want to but George is –

George is –

––––––––––––––––––––

And I find myself shouting at him.   *[burpees]*

At my dearest –

––––––––––––––––––––

At my only true –   *[burpees]*

At George.

Shouting.

––––––––––––––––––––

Shrieking.

Who does George think he is?   *[burpees]*

Drake is a friend.

You can't just –

––––––––––––––––––––

But George is adamant.   *[burpees]*

Drake doesn't get it.

But I get it, Michael.

I do.

There's no one else.

Only me.

I'm weeping now.   *[burpees]*

You have no idea how –

How –

How important friends are to someone like –

I can't just abandon them.

I can't be abandoned.

I can't be –

You think it's easy?

You think it's easy to be Steve Jobs?

Macbeth?

Magneto?

You think it's easy to be Michael Fassbender?…

George is silent for a while, before –

(Both.) You think it's easy to be me, Michael?

From now on you don't need anyone else.

George is right.

Drake is nothing.

_____

All the others are nothing.

_____

George is everything.

_____

George is good for me.

_____

George is great for me.

_____

He is.

_____

He's the best.

_____

I make him better.

_____

He improves me.

_____

My biggest fan became my best friend.

_____

My biggest fan became my –

_____

No.

Michael isn't the type.

George. Is. The. One.

Would he?

George. Is. The.

Yes.

Of course Michael would –

Of course I would do a TED talk.

About the power of –

Friends.

Friends that help.

George. Is.

Just imagine.

George.

A room full of people

Ge. Or. Ge.

Hundreds of people.

Ge. Or.

Paying to listen.

Ge.

Listening to my story.

G.

Listening to *our* story.

No.

No.

No?

No.

Again.

Again?

Again.

My biggest fan became my best friend.

My biggest fan became my best friend.

My biggest fan became my best –

My biggest fan became my –

Again.

Good evening.

Thank you to TED for inviting me to share with you all.

I hope what I have to say will be of some value.

[rest]

WWW.OBERONBOOKS.COM

Follow us on www.twitter.com/@oberonbooks
& www.facebook.com/OberonBooksLondon